JOHN SHUTTLEWORTH TAKES THE BISCUIT!

A Crumbly Selection of Songs and Stories

"Graham Fellows' genius creation is the balm we need in these troubled times. Heart-warming yet always laugh-out-loud hilarious, John Shuttleworth is the dark chocolate Digestive of British comedy - no crumbs!"

Steve Pemberton

"John Shuttleworth is one of the country's premier singer/songwriter/ storytellers. I occasionally find myself breaking into one of his songs when the mood takes me. John is one of the funniest comic creations of the last 30 years, and I laugh like a helpless child in his company."

Martin Freeman

"If you've ever been to a John Shuttleworth show and thought 'I'd love to take John out for an afternoon tea and get to know him properly'... then save the phone call, effort and money and buy this book instead!"

Lorraine Bowen (The Crumble Lady)

"It is a joy to travel through John's mind... few books that dabble anywhere near the dark arts are also so handy on hedge trimming manuals and biscuit etiquette too, making this a very useful guide to living."

Robin Ince

"John Shuttleworth has been my idol for many years for his skills as a singer-songwriter and raconteur. He makes me smile. I don't know for sure but I feel confident John is a *You and Yours* listener. Often, I imagine I am talking to John as I discuss important topics such as loft insulation."

Winifred Robinson

"John Shuttleworth's brilliant book is a sweet treat for the soul, filled with heartwarming humour. I've been chortling away since getting my flight from Aberdeen to Amsterdam. I loved it!"

Anthony Baxter

JOHN SHUTTLEWORTH TAKES THE BISCUIT!

A Crumbly Selection of Songs and Stories

OMNIBUS PRESS
London / New York / Paris / Sydney / Copenhagen / Berlin / Madrid / Tokyo

(A Division of Music Sales Limited)
14-15 Berners Street, London, W1T 3LJ)

Book designed by Amazing15
Illustrations by Kevin Baldwin

ISBN: 978-1-915-84130-8

Printed in Turkey

A catalogue record for this book is available from the British Library.

www.omnibuspress.com

Acknowledgements

Writing this book has been a complete solo effort, so I'm afraid there is nobody I need to acknowledge for helping me, and I'll thank you kindly to remember that!

Oof, I've just unintentionally thanked you all! Oh dear, I really didn't mean to. And yet, "Hang on John... it's the humble reader you've just thanked – the person who is about to go to the trouble of flicking through over 300 pages of you 'taking the biscuit!' Shouldn't you be thanking them?" Oh, I suppose so. Yes, thank you...very kind of you to give up your precious time to read my book.

Oof, you know, now I've issued one lot of thanks, I'm suddenly in the mood to thank others, so here goes… Mr Barraclough (not the governor from *Porridge* – although at times writing this I've felt like I was in jail!), he's my publisher from Omnibus Press and I just want to say... thank you David for your generous and unwavering support. Also thanks to Martin Stiff at Amazing 15 for his inspired and tireless designing, Kevin Baldwin for his terrific cartoons, Richard Bucknall for being an excellent sole agent (but don't tell Ken Worthington!), Miriam Holland for letting me borrow her laptop (but don't tell Mary as she thinks I've just been using her tablet!), Sean Bloodworth, Tony Briggs, Alan Clift, Kathryn Heywood, Steve Ullathorne and Keith Morrison for the lovely photos over the years, Mark Taylor for most of the tour flyer designs, and Milo for his weird and wonderful design of me (oof, bit arty for my liking). And a special thanks to Martin Freeman, Steve Pemberton, Lorraine Bowen, Robin Ince, Winifred Robinson and Anthony Baxter for saying extremely nice things about me and this book. Oof, not such a solo effort after all...

Contents

Introduction

You may think that in 'taking the biscuit' I must be quite greedy. Let me stress, I always offer the plate around before helping myself, unless there's only one biscuit left – in which case, I'm afraid, it's MINE! However, in extreme circumstances I *may* be prepared to share it…

I was at a children's party many years ago
The sandwiches were potted meat and the lemonade did flow…

And I spotted one biscuit left on the plate. So I said:

Shall we share the shortbread, Shirley? Surely we should!

You might also consider that someone who 'takes the biscuit' is a bit of a clown, a chump even, like my next-door neighbour and sole agent, Ken Worthington. But 'taking the biscuit' traditionally meant being the best at something, and without wanting to appear a bighead, I'm brilliant at spinning the lettuce. (Incidentally, I favour a powerful windmill action, with arm fully extended.) I'm also quite good at table tennis and win most games – even if I have the hard bat!

I'm also not bad at writing, you know, and not just song lyrics. My book boasts tons of original and fascinating stories about my life in and around Sheffield, South Yorkshire, where I reside with my charming wife, Mary Shuttleworth, and our Scottie dog, Kirsty. As for the many song lyrics (all carefully honed) contained herein, please note that they are reproduced with my kind permission… although permission didn't really need to be sought. You know, I don't mind them being included. (Indeed, I'd have been devastated if they hadn't been!)

I'm a bit rubbish at drawing though. Luckily, I know a young man (well, he's knocking on a bit now, to be fair) called Kevin Baldwin, and he's really good at drawing. He even owns his own felt-tip pens! In *John Shuttleworth Takes the Biscuit* you will find dozens of Kevin's colourful and eye-catching cartoons which illustrate some of my finest songs to date. There is even a cartoon story called *Peeping Peter*, a cautionary tale starring sleazy salesman, Peter Cornelious.

You might expect this book to contain a chapter or two about actual biscuits, and how to eat them? Oof, I'm afraid not. But I can give you some biscuit tips now, if you like? Alright then: wash your hands before you dive into the biscuit tin, and have a glass of cold milk on hand in case you choke while munching. And you should *never* use your little finger to pick up biscuits because it's just not practicable!

Finally, for the scholars out there who know that 'taking the biscuit' also means dying, or 'popping yer clogs' – after the medieval Catholic practice of 'taking the wafer' as the final sacrament – there will be candid advice from Ken Worthington, about how to prepare for your imminent death.

"No, there won't, John."

"I beg your pardon, Ken?"

"I'm sorry, but I'm not doing that. It's too macabre. Count me out, sunshine!"

"Oof, alright then, Ken, be like that!" Fret ye not, readers. We'll have an extract from my song 'From a Father to a Son' instead. It goes like this:

I will attend you when you're very ill
Plump the pillows beneath your head
I'll undertake your burial
Or my wife, Mary, will
If I'm already dead!

Oof, I hope that hasn't depressed you too much. In case it has, let me cheer you up with a short extract from another 'death' song, 'Mingling with Mourners'.

Mingling with mourners
Some sat down in corners

Others at the table eyeing up the quiche

"Oof, John. You take the biscuit, you do!"

All this talk of biscuits, I'm suddenly ravenous. Would you care to join me in 'taking a biscuit' or two, readers? You're most welcome to…

RBM PRESENTS

JOHN SHUTTLEWORTH'S GUIDE TO STARDOM

AT THE PLEASANCE UPSTAIRS

VENUE 33

FROM 14 AUGUST TO 5 SEPTEMBER AT 7.05PM

1.
The Day I Thought Ken Worthington Was the Devil

A few years ago I was with Ken Worthington at our local garden centre. We'd worked up quite an appetite in the Sheds Section. How so? Well, Ken had cavorted in the Hansel and Gretel chalet for several minutes. I don't know what he was doing in there, but his Cuban heels were making a loud clomping noise on the wooden floor. Was he performing a tap dance? As a former contestant on *New Faces* in 1973 (he came last, remember?), it's likely that he was.

"How come *you* were hungry though, John?" I hear you enquire. "We totally understand Ken becoming peckish, tap dancing as he was, but if you were only listening to Ken cavorting, why would that work up an appetite?" Incredibly good point, and I don't have the answer to it. All I was doing was sitting on a shepherd's bench (reduced from £129 to £109), an item made not from boring old wood that could splinter but from 100% polypropylene – fantastic! – and was doing absolutely nothing but listening to Ken's clomping, as you rightly point out, so… I don't know, I just don't know. Maybe I wasn't hungry. Oof, does it matter? You don't really have to be hungry to enjoy a cooked meal, do you? Well, I don't… especially at the garden centre!

Oh yes, it was smashing to sit and eat a nice hot meal in the garden centre cafeteria with my next-door neighbour and sole agent (Ken Worthington), although I can't for the life of me remember what we had to eat. Was it Russian fish pie? Probably not. They don't seem to do it since the Ukraine invasion, so it may have been lasagne with a side salad. Anyway, that's not important. What *is* crucial are the words Ken uttered as he finished his meal and put down his knife and fork, and it chills me still to think of them. He said – and please prepare yourself for this, readers – he said, "I'm Satan!"

Yes, you heard correctly. Well, no, if Ken is to be believed, you didn't hear correctly and neither did I. Upon interrogation (I wasn't going to let him get away with that!) Ken claims that he merely said, "I'm sated." Now, before you say "Hmm, that seems a reasonable explanation", just remember that Satanists and Devil Worshippers are devious and quick-thinking. Of course, he would say that's what he was saying and, to be fair, "I'm sated" does sound incredibly similar to "I'm Satan". But why didn't he behave like a normal person and say "I'm stuffed" or "I'm full as an egg" or – my favourite – "I'm full up to *here*!"? And as you say 'here' you position your hand flat across the top of your head to indicate that that's how far the food has travelled up your body. Clever idea. I don't know who first thought of that but they deserve praise for it.

But honestly, who says "I'm sated" after a big meal? Maybe someone posh like that Gyles Brandreth. I can imagine him saying that. Or Stephen Fry perhaps (although I've heard he's become a big darts fan so maybe he wouldn't say that now. Perhaps Stephen would say "I'm stuffed, mate" or "buddy". You can say 'buddy' now, which I quite like as it makes you sound like a policeman, or even a paramedic. "Keep still, buddy... relax, you're going to be just fine, buddy."). But for Ken to say "I'm sated" seems very odd to me, and anyway, he didn't say that. As I've already sated, I mean stated, he said "I'm Satan" and I recall he was grinning in a devilish way as he said it, further convincing his dining companion (me, John Shuttleworth) that he was from the land below.

After we left the garden centre, we drove home in my Austin Ambassador (Y Reg). As I drove, I tried to detect any further signs that Ken had sold his soul to 'Bezeely Bubble', is it? At one point I heard him mumbling rapidly to himself. Was he reciting the Lord's Prayer backwards? Phew, I soon realised it was just a Kenny Rogers song he was singing very badly. I arrived home and drove my Y Reg into the carport and Ken quit my vehicle and made the short journey back to his bungalow. He walked, incidentally, he didn't fly or anything (I've heard that Satan is capable of flight, you see). But it would be a very foolish devil that would do that in broad daylight knowing I was monitoring him.

And monitor him I did. Well, I tried to. It was difficult,

as he has a highbacked armchair and only the top of his bubble perm was peeking out as he sat and… well, I think he fell asleep, as his head was nodding a bit. Or was he reading out a blasphemous tract and agreeing with its sentiment? At that point Mary saw me and told me to get out of Ken's front garden and come and do some chores, so I did, and forgot all about Ken and him saying "I'm Satan" (which I'm convinced he did, you know!).

Mind you, I've dallied with the Dark Arts meself. Let me explain: I had a live show once called *The Beast of John Shuttleworth*. Oof, it was supposed to be the *The Best of John Shuttleworth*, but Ken – eager to get the copy to the printers – accidentally added an 'a' as he was typing the word 'best'. These things happen, I suppose, and at least it did allow me to explore my dark side!

The Beast of John Shuttleworth

I'm a beast. Meet the beast
The side of John Shuttleworth you know the
least
And once you do, you won't be pleased
Of work, I'm a particularly nasty piece

I broke the leg of an innocent cranefly
Devoured a seven-pack of Club biscuits in a
lay-by

(Washed down with a two-litre bottle of semi-skimmed milk!)

I'm a beast. And what a beast!
Was ever there a more villainous artiste?
For once I did feast
On an Easter egg I'd purchased for my
grandniece

I bet on a greyhound and derived pleasure
from it
I had a lustful thought about the night cleaner at
Comet

(It was only momentary… but you know, it still occurred!)

I'm a beast. Meet the beast
Ideally, I should be locked up and never released
I'm a beast, and I won't rest
till a wooden stake is driven through my chest!

(Oof, nasty! Erm, if you ever bump into my wife, Mary, I'd appreciate it if you'd keep quiet about this song, please!)

RBM Presents

The Beast of John Shuttleworth

UK Tour '97

October

Fri 31st	Romilley Forum, Stockport, 8pm, BO 0161 430 6570

November

Sun 2nd	Warwick Arts Centre, 7.30pm, BO 01203 524524
Thurs 6th	Cambridge Junction, 8.30pm, BO 01223 511511
Sat 8th	Brighton Gardner Arts Centre, 8pm, BO 01273 685861
Sun 9th	Lincoln Theatre Royal, 7.30pm, BO 01522 525555
Wed 12th	Farnham Maltings, 8pm, BO 01252 726234
Thurs 13th	Bloomsbury Theatre London, 8pm, BO 0171 388 8822
Fri 14th	Bloomsbury Theatre London, 8pm, BO 0171 388 8822
Sat 15th	Bloomsbury Theatre London, 8pm, BO 0171 388 8822
Sun 16th	Sheffield Crucible Theatre, 8pm, BO 0114 276 9922
Tues 18th	Newcastle Playhouse, 8pm, BO 0191 230 5151
Wed 19th	Bolton Albert Halls, 8pm, BO 01204 364333
Thurs 20th	Bradford St Georges Hall, 8pm, BO 01274 752672
Fri 21st	York Grand Opera House, 8pm, BO 01904 671818
Sat 22nd	Liverpool Neptune, 8pm, BO 0151 709 7844
Sun 23rd	Northampton Theatre Royal, 7.30pm, BO 01604 32533
Mon 24th	Cheltenham Town Hall, 8.30pm, BO 01242 227979
Tues 25th	Bristol Bierkeller, 8pm, BO 0117 926 8514 CC hotline 0117 929 9008
Wed 26th	Gate House Theatre, Stafford, 8pm, BO 01785 254653
Sat 29th	Kings Lynn Arts Centre, 8.30pm, BO 01553 773578
Sun 30th	Preston Charter Theatre, 7.30pm, BO 01772 258858

December

Thurs 4th	Maidstone Hazlitt Theatre, 7.30pm, BO 01622 758611
Fri 5th	Wilde Theatre, South Hill Park, 8pm, BO 01344 484123
Sun 7th	Queens Hall, Edinburgh, 8pm, BO 0131 668 2019 CC hotline 0131 667 7776

BBC Cassette and Book available from all good record and book shops.

NME

2.
A Stray Apostrophe

Before we leave the unsavoury subject of Satan, I must tell you of a misunderstanding between Ken Worthington and his (Leeds-based) client Julie Satan which will horrify some and others may find amusing. Ken was once scared witless upon receiving a harmless text message from Julie simply because it had an apostrophe where there shouldn't have been one. Let me backtrack for a second: Ken had enjoyed an evening in the company of Julie and her boyfriend Mark, who collects military memorabilia (so naturally he supplied Julie with the broadsword that features heavily in her novelty stage act). Ken had visited Julie's flat to deliver 250 promotional postcards of her dressed in a basque while holding the broadsword. (Julie's raunchy look is cleverly finished off with a leather gauntlet on one arm – upon which a stuffed falcon perches.) Once business had been taken care of, Ken shared a Chinese takeaway with the couple (would that be option C then? Meal for three persons? Oof, lovely!) and showbiz banter was exchanged. Some of it may have been of a slightly saucy nature but, Ken assures me, delivered and received in good humour by all parties. There was, at that stage, no hint of malice or evil intent.

Later, Ken drove back down the M1 in his Honda Civic to his bachelor home in a leafy suburb of Sheffield. (Oo, that makes where I live sound lovely! Ken's my next-door neighbour, you see, as I've already stated.) Once inside, Ken immediately messaged Julie and Mark thanking the couple for their hospitality, ending with a slightly risqué comment about the length of Julie's broadsword. Julie then replied with a brief text to Ken. After all, she was tired and had work in the morning (she was temping at a betting shop in Batley, you see) and was getting a bit fed up of all the silly banter with her sole agent. Still, she did her best. Her reply was in the same cheeky showbiz vein as Ken's text. She replied, "Well get you, Ken!" That's pretty harmless, in't it? Like what former *Generation Game* host Larry Grayson might have said to a cheeky contestant, or what Julie Goodyear on *Coro* might have muttered to a flustered Fred Gee, the barman (played by the late Fred Feast), except Julie Goodyear would have said "Get you, our kid!" Anyway, my point is: how could a harmless and time-honoured comment strike such fear into the heart of Ken? And yet it did, as you will soon discover.

Although Julie typed the word 'well', she had enabled the 'predictive text' function on her phone (and who doesn't these days? Erm, Alan the Opera Singer, that's who, but only because he doesn't know how to). As I was saying, predictive text was on, and it changed the word ‘well’ to something erm… slightly different. Being tired – Julie still had to make her sandwiches for next day – she failed to spot the stray apostrophe that had crept into her text message. That’s all that happened – but it was enough to wreak chaos. She pressed ‘send’, not for a second realising the damage she was about to cause and the fear she would unleash on the highly-strung impresario who – let’s not forget – as a teenager used to wake up in bed in a cold sweat every night having witnessed the apparition of a hooded axe man at the end of his bed! Oof, imagine that!

When Ken heard his phone ping (indicating the arrival of Julie’s text message) he was already in his dressing gown pouring himself a Malibu nightcap. He chuckled in anticipation of the slightly cheeky reply he assumed Julie had sent him. He picked up his phone and sat back in his armchair, still chuckling as he took a generous swig of Malibu (not a good idea to laugh as you’re consuming liquids, I would have thought… a choking hazard, wouldn’t you agree?). Ken clicked on the text message and read it. It wasn’t what he was expecting. Ken gasped in horror and began shaking. What on earth could Julie’s message mean, and why would she say those horrible words after they’d had a such lovely night and Ken had even paid for the Chinese takeaway?

You see, the message didn’t say “Well get you, Ken!” It said something far more chilling. Julie and her boyfriend Mark appeared to have decided that Ken wasn’t their friend after all, but public enemy number one, someone they had taken it upon themselves to destroy! Ken let out an involuntary moan as once more he read the evil message which said…

"WE'LL GET YOU, KEN!"

Oof, and the moral? Always check your texts before you press 'send'!

We're all suddenly in a very dark place, don't you think? I feel awful having taken you there with my spooky story. So, I feel it's my duty to get us back into the light by singing a happy little ditty all about my Scottie dog, Kirsty. Oof, I've done it again – called her a Scottie dog, when in fact she's a Westie, and always has been. Here's the song which has an uplifting 'dum-de-dum-de-dum' tune and should ideally be sung in a lilting Scottish Highland accent, with musical backing by a piper.

Kirsty Is a Westie, Not a Scottie

Kirsty is a Westie, not a Scottie
I knew that when we bought her as a puppy
But at some point I forgot
Started calling her a Scot
But she is not and must think I am potty

Kirsty's not a Scottie, she's a Westie
Mary knew but never tried to correct me
For years this joke has run
People must have thought me dumb
And Kirsty's come to shun
and even detest me

Kirsty is a Westie, not a Scottie
Everyone knew but no one tried to stop me
It's an error I regret
Repeating it to my pet
And everyone I met
While on a walkie
And to get it wrong for so long is very naughty
For Kirsty is a Westie, not a Scottie!

3. Advice for New Hedge Trimmer Owners (If They've Lost the Manual)

The curious thing is – I've also lost my manual so I'm not really in a position to give you reliable advice, sorry about that. So 'have another good look for your manual' is my first bit of advice, and I'll have a look for mine too. It's got to be somewhere!

Well, I've just looked everywhere for my manual, but I still can't find it so… hmm, as you're still reading this chapter I assume you've also looked for your manual but not found it, so you're clearly in desperate need of help. Fret ye not – I'll do my best to advise you. Forgive me if I don't remember *everything* a new hedge trimmer owner should do (it's a few years since I read my manual), but a lot of it is just common sense, you know? Firstly, you should always wear gloves, goggles and a hi-vis waistcoat when working with a hedge trimmer, although I prefer to wear a hi-vis 'tabard' as it sounds better, dun't it – *tabard*.

Incidentally, my wife Mary wears a red cloth tabard when she's working as a dinner lady at a local primary school, but that's another story. Having said that, there's not much of a story there. (Indeed, so short is the story of Mary's tabard that I reckon I've told you it in full – so back now, please, to the main story!)

All my advice is totally off the top of my head, remember, as I've lost the manual, as I've already stated. But I can remember a lot of it because I read it through three or four times when I first got the hedge trimmer. Erm… oo, that's right, I've just remembered!

'Check the hedge for foreign bodies prior to use.'

This is very important, and when Ken Worthington got a new hedge trimmer, he didn't do that. How do I know? Because he used it straight out of the box without first reading any instructions. You see, readers, I was monitoring his actions from my bedroom window (I just happened to be checking the mastic sealant on the window frame when I spotted him opening the box, lifting out the trimmer and plugging it in without reading a single word of the manual). What a crazy man. And so therefore Ken didn't bother to:

'Verify that all personnel, including children and domestic animals, are clear of the site before operating the machine.'

Actually, would that instruction be relevant to Ken? Perhaps not, as Ken is a single gentleman and without issue, and his cat died in 2003. Ah, that's sad, in't it? But Ken's a survivor, and I truly believe he is over the trauma of being divorced by former harpist Rhiannon (who, as you may know, now lives with a builder called Martin in the Derbyshire village of Stoney Middleton). But has

Ken recovered from coming last on *New Faces* in '73? Of course not, you can never get over something like that. Oh, if only he hadn't looked into the camera and made a silly face like he'd just seen a ghost...

I've just remembered some more advice. Yes, it's a good one with which to finish this section.

'Never run with a hedge trimmer!'

Not only because you might stumble and fall and snag yer tummy on one of the serrated metal blades, but because it will look like you've just stolen the trimmer and are fleeing the scene of the crime. (I made that last bit up, but it's true, would you not say?)

Right, well, in the absence of my manual – and I will keep looking – that's really all I can think of to say about using a hedge trimmer safely. I mentioned tabards a moment ago, and I'd dearly love to end this chapter with a song I wrote about another tabard. It wasn't a hi-vis tabard, but one woven from calico and worn by family friend Joan Chitty during the short period she worked as a physiotherapist. (As you'll hear in the following song, Joan developed weak wrists, so her career as a physio was cut tragically short.)

Feel free to sing lustily, even to bellow the lyrics of this one, as the number is a roundelay with a jaunty tune and tub-thumping rhythm. Enjoy!

Joan Wears a Tabard

Joan wears a tabard, a tabard, a tabard
Hangs it in a cupboard
At the end of the working day
Joan wears a tabard, a tabard, a tabard
Of which I am enamoured.
It suits her, I must say

A soldier wears a scabbard, a scabbard, a
scabbard
But Joan wears a tabard, for she is a physio
Joan wears a tabard, a tabard, a tabard
But she can't ever grab hard
Her wrists are weak and so...

She had to put the tabard, the tabard, the tabard
Back in the cupboard after a week or so
Joan wore a tabard, a tabard, a tabard
Of it I was enamoured
Worra shame it had to go
Its whereabouts I don't know
Joan's weak wrists – what a blow!
Prevented her from remaining as a physio

(That last line doesn't scan very well, I do realise that. But if you sing it very quickly it sort of fits in. Er, I can't think of any more rhymes with 'physio' – can you, readers?)

RBM Presents

John Shuttleworth

"A ludicrously compelling night out"

ALEX GAMES, EVENING STANDARD

OCTOBER			
12	ABERDEEN ARTS CENTRE	8.00 PM	Box Office: 01224 641122
18	GRAND OPERA HOUSE, YORK	8.00 PM	Box Office: 01904 671818
19	WYVERN THEATRE, SWINDON	8.00 PM	Box Office: 01793 524481
24	THE JUNCTION, CAMBRIDGE	8.00 PM	Box Office: 01223 511511
25	THE GANTRY, SOUTHAMPTON	8.00 PM	Box Office: 01703 229319
26	DANCEHOUSE, MANCHESTER	8.00 PM	Box Office: 0161 237 9753
27	OLD REP, BIRMINGHAM	7.30 PM	Box Office: 0121 236 5622
28	CHELTENHAM TOWN HALL	8.30 PM	Box Office: 01242 227979
31	CITY VARIETIES MUSIC HALL, LEEDS	8.00 PM	Box Office: 0113 243 0808
NOVEMBER			
1	NEPTUNE THEATRE, LIVERPOOL	8.00 PM	Box Office: 0151 709 7844
3	PLAYHOUSE THEATRE, NEWCASTLE	8.00 PM	Box Office: 0191 230 5151
6	SPRING STREET THEATRE, HULL	8.00 PM	Box Office: 01482 323638
10	THEATRE ROYAL, LINCOLN	7.30 PM	Box Office: 01522 525555/534570
12-16	BLOOMSBURY THEATRE, LONDON	8.00 PM	Box Office: 0171 388 8822

"Do not miss"

THE SUNDAY TIMES

Single out soon

4. I Was Wary of George Clarke (and Other TV Star Observations)

Initially, I was a bit resistant to watching the TV show *George Clarke's Amazing Spaces* because I thought the presenter – George Clarke – was a ne'er-do-well. Mind you, I once felt the same about Radio 2's Vernon Kay, not to mention that lad who presents that show with all the lasses who have to keep their light on if they want to go on a date. But in both cases – once I'd heard them crack a few jokes in their cosy Lancastrian burr – I relaxed and warmed to their oafish appeal. As for George Clarke, on first inspection he's a bit more sophisticated, granted, but I noticed his hands were thrust deep into his pockets and he was sniggering a lot, as if guilty of some wrongdoing. What made things worse was that it sounded like he had a bad cold, and yet at no point did George produce a hanky or get out his nasal spray or tell the viewers that it would soon be time to take his medicine. So, initially at least, yes, I was *very* wary of George Clarke.

However, as he climbed into an old ice cream van and looked around the 'amazing space' – still grinning, still sounding very nasal, with no hanky on show – Mary pointed out that he was sporting a lovely leather jacket. I looked and thought. "Mmm, so he is. Oof, that leather jacket's even more eye-catching than Lovejoy's!" And so it was. There was lots of ribbing on the shoulders and upper sleeves giving it an excellent 'Armadillo' quality. Have you ever seen it, readers? It is really eye-catching is George's jacket, and it certainly gives Lovejoy's a run for its money.

Despite the fab jacket… I remained dubious. Was it wise to watch an unknown show with a ne'er-do-well presenter in its entirety, or should we tune into *Dogs Behaving (Very) Badly*? Clever marketing that – sticking a 'Very' in the title (just as the 'Amazing' in George Clarke's show is clever, but, hey, we'll come on to that). *Dogs Behaving (Very) Badly* – hosted by the charismatic Graeme Hall – had only just started airing, but Mary's friend, Joan Chitty, whose budgie Les had died just before the first pandemic and who had needed something to help distract her – alerted us to the show, and to Graeme's incredible powers. Nothing dodgy-looking about Graeme, of course. Joan forewarned me that he wore a tight jean that favoured him well, and indeed it does. Joan strongly recommended that I buy exactly the same style and brand of jeans. "Well, I'd love to, Joan," I told Joan, "but short of contacting Graeme and asking him what brand they are, how on earth will I find that out?"

You see… Graeme favours a tweed jacket (which you could argue is a little old-fashioned. Wouldn't he be better off with a slip-on fleece that he could just chuck in the wash after all those dogs have been slobbering over him?). My point is this: the tweed jacket covers the waistband of his jeans where the label sits, so I don't know what brand they are. Having said that, once Graeme bent right over to reprimand a naughty poodle and I was nearly able to read the label. The thing is – despite Joan pressurising me to switch – I'm quite happy with my stretch snow-washed denim jeans that Mary bought me in 2013 from a catalogue. Yes, they're baggier than Graeme's, which are rather tight on the thigh, I notice. I wear my 'snowy' jeans rarely, so there's still plenty of life left in them. Having said that, there's a fleck of paint on the right knee that even vigorous scrubbing with a turpy rag won't shift, so perhaps I should get in contact with Graeme. I could ask him where he gets his neckerchief from an' all, as I suspect Ken Worthington might be interested in purchasing one!

Oof, I'm straying off the point again, but this time... only slightly. You see, George Clarke wears tight jeans too, as I recall (but, sadly, he doesn't sport a neckerchief like Graeme's), although before we carry on with Clarkey let's consider for a moment the appeal of Kevin McCloud on *Grand Designs*. He's been known to sport a tight jean on occasion, although once I saw him in big baggy pants, like a clown might wear. (I'm sure Leo Sayer used to wear them in the eighties – not Kevin's pair, they'd be far too big for Little Leo!)

He's a bit snooty, would you not say, that Kevin McCloud? And at the end of the show he sits and talks for ages with the couple who, against all the odds, have managed to finish the house that they didn't think they ever would. Instead of chatting, Kev should be examining the fabric of the new building. He should be out with a spirit level checking if the worktop is true, opening and closing doors to see if they fit properly. Shame on you, Kevin, for ducking your responsibilities in that way! But oof... credit where it's due – I notice Kevin always wears a hard hat and hi-vis tabard when making onsite visits. Good on yer, Kev!

But back to Clarkey... Oof, I hope George isn't offended by me calling him that. He seems quite good-natured, so I imagine he'd just grin and say, "You can call me what you like, Mr Shuttleworth... within reason!" And then he'd let out a big laugh, because, yes, he seems a decent fella. Not a ne'er-do-well at all, I don't know why I said that. (You can tell I'm warming to Clarkey now, can't you?!) So anyway, after consulting with my wife, we decided 'tight jean' Graeme Hall (or for short... Halley? Oof no, that's a comet, or an orchestra. Let's stick with Graeme) would have to wait his turn. Mary and I decided tonight was the night we were going to commit to watching a whole show with Clarkey.

I was in my armchair, and Mary was on the sofa with her legs tucked up as ladies seem to like to do nowadays. Twenty years ago I don't think that posture was so prevalent, but it certainly is now, isn't it, girls? Like myself, Mary was a little bit sniffy at first about watching a whole episode of Clarkey, not just because of the lure of Graeme and his jeans and neckerchief (and his waistcoat, I forgot to mention that!), but because she prefers *Holidays in the Sun* or *Four in a Bed*. But soon she realised – as did I – that not only does Clarkey have a lovely Armadillo jacket, but his spaces really are AMAZING! Whoever thought of that title *George Clarke's Amazing Spaces* should receive a pat on the back because they got it bang on! They *are* amazing spaces, and George, sorry, Clarkey constantly reminds the viewers that they are amazing by saying "that's amazing!" every few seconds, which cleverly reinforces the title.

Sometimes Clarkey says "that's fantastic" or "it's brilliant" or "incredible", which gives the show variety and keeps the audience on their toes. At one point he said, "That's so cool", which I thought was shrewd as it would help him to appeal to the all-important younger viewer. He's the consummate presenter in my view, in't he, George Clarke? Hmm, or is he? I've just remembered… now and again he'll say a space is 'unbelievable', which I don't think is very helpful. You see, the viewers are struggling as it is to believe that these spaces could've been created out of an old shed and a few bits of wood, and then he goes and says, "That is unbelievable!" Well, it makes you suspicious and think "No, I don't believe it either. It's probably trick photography!" Or AI, which is coming through strong now, so I'm led to believe.

Another thing I don't like Clarkey saying is "I can't wait to see this!", which suggests an immaturity and a lack of patience he should try to curb. He needs to work on that, do you not think? It would be better if he said "Take your time, take your time…", just like Jim Bowen used to do on *Bullseye*, although that was a foolish thing to say (I hope Jim won't mind me saying that, if he's looking down from Heaven right now, which I'm sure he is) because it would be near the end of the programme when he said "Take your time, take your time" and there was actually very little time. Instead of saying "Take your time", Jim should have yelled "Get on with it! Chuck those arrows as fast as you can – there's a good girl" if it was a lady, although generally it was a bloke, so he should have said "Hurry up, buddy!", although, sadly, the word 'buddy' wasn't in common usage back then.

Jim also said "Listen to Tony", which was better advice as Tony was a very wise man and worthy of being listened to. Well, I don't know that he was wise, but he certainly looked it, and he was good at adding up quickly, which at the end of the show was essential. My only criticism of Tony is this: sometimes he stood too close to the dartboard and 'sideways on', which with his big tummy wasn't wise, surely? He was liable to be speared by a stray dart!

Back to Clarkey… At the end of the episode we watched, he said of the space he'd created, "This is truly stupendous", which I simply couldn't agree with. I thought it was 'truly stupid' and I'd have preferred it if they'd kept it as an ice cream van with an ability to dispense 99s and Mivvies on a hot summer's day. But Mary was nodding in agreement with Clarkey, so what do I know? Then I noticed Mary reach for a sip of her red wine, which is like what a Roman goddess would have done, I suppose. Mary is a goddess to me, and I'd love to make *her* an amazing space myself one day. Because I'm quite good at DIY, if I say so myself. (Although I don't 'take the biscuit' at it like I do at lettuce-spinning!). But it would be truly stupendous if I could make Mary an amazing space – really fantastic and oh so cool! Oof, I'm doing it now… talking like Clarkey. Maybe I could take over from him as the show's presenter if he's ever poorly? Hey, it might happen if his cold gets worse and he doesn't have any nasal spray to hand. I'd love to present the show… as long as I get my petrol money and am allowed to borrow that Armadillo jacket!

Unfortunately, I haven't got a song about amazing spaces with which to end this chapter, but I do have one about red wine, which I've mentioned Mary was quaffing in a goddess-like fashion. I'm not sure about red wine myself – it looks a bit funny, like you could be drinking blood – but I've heard it's quite pleasant. Ken Worthington – when he's not guzzling Malibu – likes a glass or two of vino, and he's partial to a Hobnob biscuit also. Now I get that, but consuming them both together, which Ken did one hot summer's day, is just plain weird.

Red Wine and Hobnobs

Red wine and Hobnobs
In Ken's living room
It feels like Christmas
In the middle of June
And he's still not dressed
Just underpants and vest
The house is a mess
But Ken has confessed
He couldn't care less

Red wine and Hobnobs
In Ken's living room
He's getting tired
He thinks he'll lie down soon
He puts the TV on
And watches Wimbledon
Lendl won
He shouldn't have done
Another hour gone...

Red wine and Hobnobs
Oh, what a crying shame
Think of the odd jobs
Ken could have done that day!
"Ken? Were you depressed?"
"Maybe a little, yes

But I didn't mind
I had a lovely time
It was a very nice wine
And I feel a sense of loss
For the day I was
Undressed and unwashed"

(Oof, that's rather worrying – that Ken should feel like that. Honestly, Ken, what a foolish man you are. As I've already stated – you take the biscuit, you do, and I don't just mean a whole packet of Hobnobs!)

I'm relieved that last song wasn't accompanied by a cartoon strip, as it would have subjected you, dear reader, to the unpleasant sight of Ken Worthington in his underpants. However, you're about to see a cartoon strip of a song about Ken experiencing tummy troubles, so it's almost as bad, and you must expect that unsavoury images will appear. I'm sorry – avert your gaze if you must. But that would be a shame as you'll miss the hilarious cartoon drawings from the amazing pen of Kevin Baldwin. It's the first of several offerings from Kevin in this book, and it's an old favourite song of mine (but not of Ken's, I suspect).

5.
Eggs and Gammon

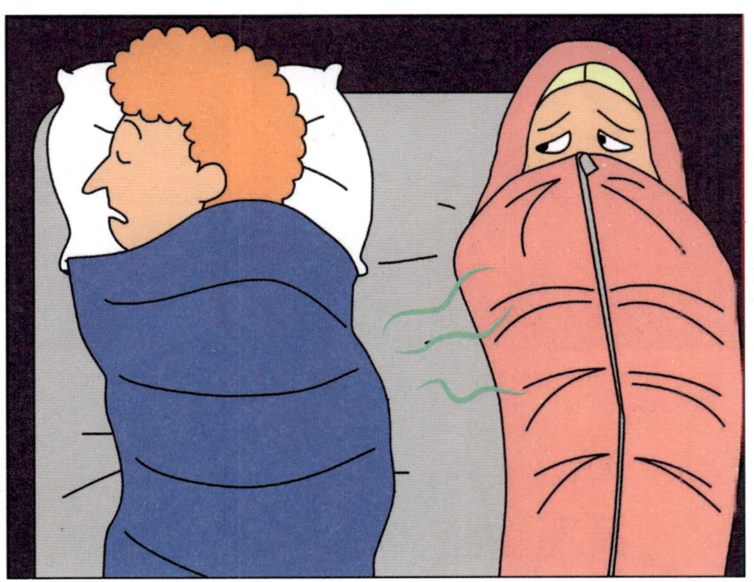

KEN HAD SOME EGGS AND GAMMON
AT A RESTAURANT IN RHYL.

THEY OPENED UP
THE TENT FLAPS ,
BUT THE SMELL -
IT SEEMED TO STAY.

THEY TIGHTENED ALL THE GUY ROPES
JUST IN CASE THEY BLEW AWAY.

THEY SAW A
DADDY LONGLEGS
GET ON HIS
KNEES AND PRAY.

EGGS AND GAMMON,
POOR RHIANNON - KEN HAD WIND.
EGGS AND GAMMON,
POOR RHIANNON - KEN'S BAD WIND.

AND IN THE MORNING,
THE STORM, IT DID SUBSIDE.

EGGS AND GAMMON,
POOR RHIANNON – KEN HAD WIND.
EGGS AND GAMMON,
POOR RHIANNON – KEN'S BAD WIND.

John Shuttleworth

in

If music be the love of food – tuck in!

Pleasance

Box office 0131 556 6550

8-20 August 7.30pm

with special guest **Brian Appleton**

"A ***tour de force*** of comic observation"

THE TIMES

An 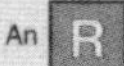   presentation

6.
A Ladle Fable

I do like a bowl of soup, and I always hope that it's been placed in the bowl by means of a ladle. Obviously, if I'm having my soup in a garden centre or cafe where the kitchen's out of public view, I can't verify that it's been ladled into the bowl. Is that frustrating? Of course it is, but I don't let it get to me. At motorway service stations I notice nowadays you can serve yourself, and the ladle is left in or on top of the tureen for members of the public to use, trusting that they won't steal it. Isn't it marvellous that they trust us not to steal the ladle? Why would they not? Well, because the ladle is a very desirable kitchen utensil and I'll never forget the day that we couldn't find ours. Between you and me, I fervently believed it had been stolen – and it sort of had.

My wife Mary had made some celery soup. I beg your pardon, it was leek and potato. (They're a very similar colour, aren't they, so the confusion can arise.) I'd already washed my hands and was sat at the table eagerly waiting for Mary to serve it up. But she couldn't find the ladle.

After a time, I got up and helped her look. We looked everywhere but we just couldn't locate it. The mood was tense: I made helpful suggestions as to the ladle's possible whereabouts, but they all seemed to make Mary tense up. With every new suggestion she got angrier, and her face more flushed. So I kept my comments to a minimum as we continued the search in miserable silence.

Eventually, Mary let out a big sigh and said, "It doesn't matter, John. I'll just spoon it out…" Well, as I have already stated, I like my soup to be placed in the soup bowl by a ladle, and I felt as sick as a dog knowing that it wasn't going to be. But Mary couldn't even find a big spoon, so in the end she just poured the soup from the saucepan directly into the bowls. Slopped it in, she did. I love my wife dearly, but at that moment I felt a bit ashamed of her crudely sloshing soup from the pan. Inevitably, some missed the bowls and landed on the worktop. Well, I had to look away, it was awful, and I'll be honest, readers, I didn't really enjoy my bowl of soup that day – knowing it had been slopped into the bowl by a rather irate lady (Mary Shuttleworth, my wife) rather than ladled in a relaxed manner by a calm woman (my wife again, obviously, but when she's not all stressed like she was then).

A postscript to this sorry tale: we *did* find the ladle. Our son Darren had borrowed it to spoon hot water onto his car windscreen during a recent cold snap, and then had foolishly put it in the boot of his Vauxhall Astra. Silly lad, and irresponsible in not returning the ladle to the kitchen immediately. Stern words were had! You'll be pleased to know that it's now back in the drawer, although its place there is threatened. "How so?" you may enquire. Well, that ladle often now seems to make the drawer jam, riding up as it does and hindering the previously smooth action of the drawer. I'm sure the drawer can't have shrunk in height or the ladle grown in size, so it's a mystery waiting to be solved. I've set aside an hour next Tuesday morning after breakfast to try and fathom just exactly what's going on!

While I've got my toolbox out, I'll probably use my spirit level to check our mug tree for levelness and general stability. Once it was rickety and all over the place and the situation was so serious that, yes, I just had to write a song about it…

The Mug Tree

I place the kettle on its base
And push the button down
Check the red light's glowing
So I know the kettle's going
Reach for the mug tree and despite
Spinning it round and round
My favourite mug is nowhere to be found

I choose another mug and wonder
Why the kettle's taking ages
Pour out some of the water
So the boiling cycle's shorter
Put the teabag in the mug
One of the key stages
There's many more to come, of course,
Some of them quite dangerous!

Oof... a problem with the mug tree
Is diverting my attention
No mugs on one side, meaning
The mug tree's badly leaning
I hear a click, the kettle's boiled
And suddenly there's tension
A dozen things require my intervention

I've just spied my favourite mug

Upon the draining board
Should I use it now for my tea?
Or to balance up the mug tree?
Meanwhile, the milk needs opening
I'd forgotten that, oh Lord,
These tasks take time that I can ill afford!

The mug tree's my priority
Though I've a thirst to kill
And so – taking no chances –
I empty all the branches
Then carefully and evenly
The mug tree I refill
Until it is perfectly vertical

I check this with a spirit level
Though it isn't necessary
I'm confident, even cocky,
That my mug tree won't be rocky
Pleased as punch, I show the mug tree
To my wife – "Look, Mary!
Let's celebrate with a 'cafeteeairy'!"

(We didn't want a cup of tea any more. It had taken so long to make the mug tree vertical, it was coffee time!)

7. How to Dress for the Seaside

Here in the UK we *can't* ever guarantee the weather will be fine, so when you're embarking on a day trip to anywhere – and especially the seaside – I do urge you to pack your kagoule (as well as your swimming togs). And you may decide to wear long trousers instead of shorts. And have you popped a thick sweater in your holdall? You have? Good thinking! If you're in a skirt today, I'd advise woolly tights should be packed in case the weather turns. (Notice I didn't say "if you are a lady, I advise you to pack woolly tights" – our Karen says it's illegal now to say that as some gentlemen might want to sport a skirt and pair of woolly tights.) Oof, well, anything goes nowadays, so I'm told.

If I were going to the seaside – as I inevitably do when I check Ken's chalet at Sutton-on-Sea, Lincs – I would tend to put on shorts, but I'll don them warily and have a pair of long trousers on standby, just in case. Shorts are all very well when it's hot and sunny, but a sudden temperature drop or exposure to a steady sea breeze can leave the shorts wearer vulnerable and anxious. I remember many years ago attending an event in a pair of shorts, and it wasn't a pleasant experience. Shall I tell you all about that? "Yes, please!" I suspect many readers are hollering. Well, I appreciate your interest in wanting to learn about yet another episode in my eventful life. I just hope you don't regret being so curious! Very well… here goes!

It was a good few years ago, as I've already stated, a period when I was a single gentleman working at Comet demonstrating audio equipment. A colleague had invited me to his weekend barbecue, and as it was a nice sunny day I decided to wear a pair of shorts for the occasion. However, later on as evening approached it got decidedly chilly and people started wandering into the house. I remained in the garden next to the barbecue – trying to extract any residual heat left in the coals' embers. There was very little, and my legs became increasingly cold. "Why didn't you go inside with the others and get warm, John?" you may wonder in a concerned tone. I'd forgotten to bring my long trousers to change into, that's why. I'd have been the only one inside dressed in shorts and, as I recall, those shorts were quite tight on the thigh, so I might have felt a bit self-conscious. I decided to remain in the garden next to the barbie.

I distracted myself by retrieving a couple of burgers that had fallen through the barbecue grill into the drip tray. I could see them poking out from a big pile of ash, and it seemed a great shame to leave them. Before you say "Oo, John, yer dirty devil doing that… those burgers were contaminated!", please remember that those burgers had been preserved in the ash, in a similar fashion to the bodies that were buried when Mount Vesuvius erupted in Up Pompeii many years previously. (I'd read all about that in the *Reader's Digest* only days before as I waited at the dentist's for a check-up.) And those burgers had only been there an hour or two, so they'd surely have been much fresher than the bodies found in Pompeii? Anyhow, once the ash coating had been removed – not an easy job as a lot of ash had been absorbed into the excess burger fat – they tasted not too bad. Put it this way – I managed one and a half before I started to feel a tad queasy. But the point is this: distracting myself with an activity allowed me to cope with being in the garden in shorts and extend the period I could endure the freezing evening air.

A few days later, I began composing a song all about my experience in the chilly garden. The composition was never finished and remains a fragment, but, hey, why don't I sing it now to give you an idea of its potential?

Vulnerable in My Shorts

I feel vulnerable, vulnerable,
vulnerable in my shorts
The wind might blow, and before I know,
a cold I could have caught
Vulnerable, vulnerable,
vulnerable in my shorts
And I really didn't ought
to feel vulnerable in my shorts!
Long trousers I should have brought!
A harsh lesson I've been taught!

(Lots of rhymes with 'shorts' are needed here as the song becomes increasingly frantic and strident. Feel free to make up your own rhymes, although – as with the Tabard song – I can't think of any more, sorry!)

RBM PRESENTS

JOHN SHUTTLEWORTH

IN

Ken's Karvery

1999 TOUR

"A TOUR DE FORCE OF COMIC OBSERVATION"

CLIVE DAVIS, THE TIMES

"PUNCH THE AIR TO CHARACTER COMEDY IN A CLASS OF ITS OWN"

HELEN HAWKINS THE SUNDAY TIMES

When I've got round to recording that one, I might send a cassette copy to our old friend, Leo Sayer. Little Leo has the personality and physicality required to do that song justice. You see, 'Vulnerable' will require a fairly aggressive delivery, accompanied by foot stomping and even fist punching too. A group like the Wurzels in their heyday would have made a superb job of it, and – who knows – even enjoyed a number one smash with 'Vulnerable'. Doh... too late now! Or… (just thinking outside the box for a moment) what about Bronski Beat? You remember that lad with a high voice who looked like Tintin? Yes, he'd have done it brilliantly too. But both combos have gone dreadfully quiet, so, erm… I might have to send it to Michael Ball. If he doesn't want to record it, I could try Michael Bublé? Not Michael Parkinson as he's sadly no longer around… hmm… Michael Owen? The former Liverpool footballer might be looking for a new career. Hey, I sense we're getting fixated on the name Michael. It could be sung by anybody with any name and that includes the ladies. Oo… Michaela Strachan?

Doh, I've just remembered – I've run out of Oxygen cassette tapes and they're a bit pricey and hard to get hold of. Also, I've heard they're highly biased, which puts you off, dun't it? And I'd have to go to the post office to buy a new Jiffy bag so… I dunno… I might not bother. We'll see. Leave it with me, please.

Listen, we seem to have run out of hints on 'How to dress for the seaside'. I apologise, but at the same time I'm not going to beat myself up about it. You had a few useful tips at the beginning and you got to hear a powerful (albeit unfinished) song about being vulnerable in your shorts. I'll keep thinking, and I'd appreciate it if you'd do the same. Oof, I've just remembered in time… flip flops – don't forget to pack them. And some two pence coins, for if you want to pop to the amusement arcade for a flutter.

This chapter has already featured a song, but as it was only a fragment it doesn't really count. Besides, I mentioned Sutton-on-Sea at the start so let's end with a rendition of a composition about that classy Lincolnshire village. The words are by yours truly, but it uses a tune written by a lovely chap called Gordon Giltrap. If you're not familiar with Gordon's work, he does finger-picking on guitar, so in that sense his style is very similar to that of my stablemate, Janet Le Roe. However, as far as I'm aware, Gordon doesn't yet have a residency at a Toby Inn. But keep plugging away, Gordon, and one day it might happen for you!

Sutton-on-Sea

Come with me
To Sutton-on-Sea
It will be terrific
A sea as calm as
Judith Chalmers
We will have a lovely time
Subject to the weather being fine

Come with me
To Sutton-on-Sea
We can have a picnic
On the beach
Two sandwiches each
More if you are really hungry, but
Save room for some biscuits and yoghurt!

Come with me
To Sutton-on-Sea
It will be terrific
A sea as calm as
Judith Chalmers
We will have a lovely time
Subject to the weather being fine

(Of course, it'll probably chuck it down, so don't forget to pack that kagoule!)

2000 & JOHN

with special guest

BRIAN APPLETON

'WONDERFUL TRAGI-COMIC SPOOF' The Independent

Date	Time	Venue	Phone
17 March	8.00pm	Warwick Arts Centre COVENTRY	024 7652 4524
18 March	7.30pm	Charter Theatre PRESTON	01772 258 858
19 March	7.45pm	Theatre Royal BRIGHTON	01273 328 488
21 March	8.00pm	Neptune LIVERPOOL	0151 709 7844
22 March	8.00pm	Town Hall LOUGHBOROUGH	01509 231 914
23 March	8.00pm	City Varieties LEEDS	0113 243 0808
25 March	7.30pm	Crucible SHEFFIELD	0114 249 6000
26 March	7.30pm	Crucible SHEFFIELD	0114 249 6000
29 March	8.00pm	Grand Opera House YORK	01904 671 818
30 March	8.00pm	Assembly Rooms DERBY	01332 255 800
31 March	8.00pm	Corn Exchange CAMBRIDGE	01223 357 851
1 April	8.00pm	Palace Theatre NEWARK	01636 655 755
2 April	7.30pm	Opera House MANCHESTER	0161 242 2509
7 April	8.00pm	Shepherd's Bush Empire LONDON	0207 771 2000
8 April	8.00pm	Gantry SOUTHAMPTON	01703 229 319
9 April	8.00pm	Bierkeller BRISTOL	0117 926 8514 / 929 9008

PHOTOGRAPHY: SHAUN BLOODWORTH

8.
I Fell Asleep Watching Judge John Deed!

One night I started watching *Judge John Deed* starring the charismatic actor Martin Shaw and fell fast asleep! How could this happen? What on earth was going on? Granted, I'd had an early start that morning. Mary had needed a lift to the dentist's first thing and prior to that I had to wheel a wheelie bin down our path – negotiating a difficult bend where a shrub sticks out – ready for collection. Later that morning I helped Ken move some patio flags in his garden, which puffed me out a bit. And then I had to spin the lettuce in our garden at teatime, which was more physical exertion, but I didn't mind because I love employing the windmill action required to spin the lettuce and – without wishing to appear big-headed – I am rather good at spinning it. (I think I mentioned this in the intro too, so mentioning it twice does seem a little conceited, I admit. Then again, it's not healthy to hide your light under a bushel, is it?) I tend to spin the lettuce for a full seven to eight minutes – but why, you ask, when the water droplets cease to be jettisoned from the spinner after about two minutes? Better to be safe than sorry, I say! So, after that task I was shattered, but my duties weren't over. Next, I had to eat my tea, which was quiche and baked potato with a side salad including (overly dry, oof!) lettuce. What's tiring about that? Well, the skin of the jacket potato was pretty tough, so I had to expend a lot of energy sawing it up with my knife.

After tea I helped Mary clear the table and load the dishwasher, and then I had to go round the house (which involved mounting and descending the stairs) closing all the curtains, tucking them (where applicable) behind the radiators to minimise heat loss. So, when it came to settling down with *Judge John Deed* on the sofa, I was – as you can imagine – utterly shattered. But to actually fall asleep during such a gripping legal drama (and it was after about two minutes – the programme had barely got going) is embarrassing. I couldn't believe it and was quite angry with myself. Especially as Mary nudged me twice, apparently, to offer me a Roses chocolate, but I was away with the fairies. And if Martin Shaw ever happened to read this, then he'd have every reason to be furious with me. (Oof… if you are reading this Martin, "Greetings, sirrah, and thanks so much for choosing to buy my book! Let's meet up socially at some point soon!")

If this Rip Van Winkle behaviour had been a one-off incident, I could have forgiven myself. But would you believe it? The following week I was watching *Dalziel and Pascoe* and exactly the same thing happened. This time I hadn't been spinning the lettuce or lifting patio slabs, so I had no excuses. Besides, I'd have thought that the slightly scary face and voice – raspy and snarling in tone – of the late Warren Clarke (Detective Superintendent Andy Dalziel in the gutsy TV crime drama) would have kept me wide awake throughout the programme, wouldn't you? This is certainly the case when I watch *Death in Paradise*, in the episodes which feature that lad with the funny stare. Do you know the one I mean? He looks like he's seen a ghost (as did Ken Worthington, of course, when he came last on *New Faces* in '73) and I reckon that's why I don't doze off during his episodes – you're kept continually alert in case a ghost suddenly appears. Having said that, don't the waves continually lapping on the Caribbean island shore have a soporific effect? Yes, they do, and to be fair I have nearly nodded off during the beach scenes.

Why am I becoming so prone to dozing while watching top TV shows? I don't know, frankly, and was hoping you might be able to tell me why. No? You don't know? Alright then, I'll have to suggest a couple of theories: the first is that I'm no spring chicken and our settee is rather comfy, especially in the evening after I've had a big tea. Another theory is this: it's because these days I'm used to watching a lot of shows that Mary likes – crime and medical dramas that contain strong language and which are 'hard-hitting from the outset'. Because of this, whenever I watch anything a bit gentler without loads of violence and nasty language, I start to relax and this can induce the state of sleep. What do you think, readers?

Watching the last Olympics I dozed off quite a lot, as

some of the sports were very easy on the eye, like cycling and rowing, with soothing scenery in the background. I remember one day waking up from a snooze to see an interview on the telly with one of our Olympic rowers and I noticed he was sporting a topknot like Gareth Bale, the Welsh footballer. Darren's friend, Plonker, sported one for a few weeks last summer, and I have to say it made him seem like he had special powers. How so? Well, it's association, in't it? Because that genie, Shazzan – the kids' cartoon series from the late sixties – he had a topknot. Well, it might have been a ponytail, but in my head it seems like a topknot (or man bun, as my daughter Karen calls them. She's assured me that's the correct term, you know, she's not having a laugh at my expense). Shazzan also often had his arms folded, which seems a bit rude, but not if you're a genie. A lot of footballers do that nowadays when they're lining up or posing for photos, and as a lot of them are like Gareth with topknots (or man buns) it gives our young professional footballers a magical 'genie' quality – smashing!

Anyway, I can't remember what that episode of *Judge John Deed* was about. Hardly surprising, as Martin Shaw hadn't done much apart from walk into a building carrying a briefcase before I nodded off. But what happened then? I really want to know. (I've asked Mary who watched the whole thing, but she can't remember either!) Did he drop the briefcase on the way in? Was it snatched from his grasp by a villain posing as a court official? Did the building suddenly collapse on Martin, burying him alive?

If so, I suspect quick thinking on Martin's part – placing his briefcase over his head – would have saved him! Oof, I'm suddenly dead keen to watch the episode I missed. But how the heck will I find it? I don't know about you, but there's just so many TV series, serials, box sets, etc out there, it's impossible to keep on top of them and know when you've watched them all. Mary seems to know because she 'binge watches' and she's always pressing the 'stream now' button. But I can't be bothered, and to be honest, I miss the gentle voices of TV in the past, like Johnny Morris on *Animal Magic* or Tony Hart on *Vision On*. Now we have Judge Judy shouting at everyone to "sit down, stand up, shut up!" She's too dictatorial and it puts you on edge.

I miss the simplicity of television back in the early days of colour. When there were only two channels – beg your pardon, BBC Two had just started, so there were three. But there was no Channel 4 or 5, and no shopping channels – how did we survive? To be honest, there wasn't much on to watch and nothing of note on BBC Two. That was the snooty station back then – before *Pot Black* (the snooker show) began airing, which made it attractive to the ordinary viewer, especially if you had a colour set, which we didn't. It was just *Open University* and other boring programmes that would have definitely sent me to sleep, if I'd ever bothered to watch them. My favourite thing on BBC Two was the testcard with that lass on (she had a topknot, didn't she, that lass… or was it a high ponytail? It gave her a slight genie quality, I suppose...) I used to watch that testcard for ages just in case the clown moved.

Once my mother took me to an old lady's house with a colour telly, and while they were out of the room looking at her new twin tub washing machine, I got up close to the TV screen and examined the separate dots, which were green, red and blue. I just couldn't understand how red and green made yellow, because if you mixed them as paints you'd get a very dark brown. But, listen, before I get too technical, let's end the chapter with an old song of mine which celebrates those early days of colour TV. Most of the song is spoken, but there's a tiny bit that's sung, which just happens to be the title!

Brightness, Contrast and Colour

(Spoken over a jaunty rhumba track)

Most people in the nineteen sixties had television sets, but they were black and white, and viewing was a hit-and-miss affair. The horizontal hold kept going, and often we'd find ourselves on the roof adjusting the aerial. Those with coin-operated sets had their own particular problems: I remember missing the end of an exciting Mick McManus bout on Saturday Wrestling *because I'd run out of shillings. Ha, I never did find out how Mick fared in that contest. Primitive though conditions were, we still had some control over our lives. We had brightness, contrast, but at that stage... no colour.*

One evening in the late sixties when I was walking past a local guesthouse, I saw – through a chink in the curtains – a colour transmission of the BBC flagship production, War and Peace. *The sight of a young Anthony Hopkins resplendent in a bright blue tunic holding aloft a glass of port with all its subtle crimson shades convinced me that I just had to make the switch to colour. But it was pricey, very pricey, and secondhand sets were hard to come by. So, although there was a light at the end of the tunnel, we were still some way off from owning...*

Brightness, contrast and colour!
Brightness, contrast and colour!
Brightness, contrast and colour!

It was a great day indeed when I paid the first instalment on a repossessed ITT 26-inch colour set. It took three grown men to unload the beast from a colleague's Ford Zephyr, but at last I'd realised my dream...

Brightness, contrast and colour!
Brightness, contrast and colour!
Brightness, contrast and colour!

RBM PRESENTS

JOHN SHUTTLEWORTH

has

One Foot in the Gravy

"PUNCH THE AIR TO CHARACTER COMEDY IN A CLASS OF IT'S OWN"

Helen Hawkins, The Sunday Times

"A LUDICROUSLY COMPELLING NIGHT OUT"

Alexander Games, Evening Standard

With special guest

BRIAN APPLETON

9. A Tatty Story

'Tats' is short for 'potatoes', isn't it? No, it's not – it's short for 'tattoos', and nowadays everybody has 'tats' it seems, except me and my wife Mary. We're not interested in marking our bodies so permanently, thank you very much, but you go ahead if you're so inclined. Each to their own, I say. Our daughter Karen has a couple of tats, and what about her flatmate, Maxine? Well, I don't know, it's none of my business – or yours, if you don't mind me saying. But Karen told me something recently that (at the risk of betraying a confidence) I feel I have to mention…

Maxine has changed her name to Morag. Why? Well, because it makes her sound like a witch! A white witch – that's what she wants to be, apparently, according to our Karen. I find that utterly baffling and very sad, because Maxine is currently a successful veterinary technician. Still, if we're to take Maxine (sorry... Morag) seriously, then I presume if she has any 'tats' they'll be of cats and broomsticks? Oof, I shouldn't make light of it. If I displease Morag she might turn me into a frog! Oof, perish the thought! Let's get back to the tatty story ASAP!

Where were we? Although 'tats' is not an acceptable abbreviation for the popular vegetable, 'tatties' is. However, I've never been that keen on 'tatties' – it sounds a bit too Scottish for my liking. Oof, apologies to readers from North of the Border if that last comment caused offence… I'm delighted you've joined us. Keep reading and feel free to continue saying 'tatties'! Another abbreviation is 'spud', but Mary's not keen on that one. Also, I don't know if you agree, readers, but isn't there a slight risk that the 's' of 'spud' might be ignored? For example: What if the 's' is mistaken for a shred of rolling tobacco that's become stuck to your shopping list? If that happens, you'll end up buying lots of 'puds' – treacle sponges or apple tartlets, that sort of thing. (Nothing wrong with that, some would argue!)

The correct abbreviation of 'potatoes' and the one always used on our shopping lists is 'pots'. My mother used to write 'pots' on all her lists and would send me out to the local shops with confidence, knowing I would correctly interpret the word 'pots' as potatoes and bring back a hearty bagful every time. As a bachelor I was comfortable with it, and as a married man too I have always enjoyed using that abbreviation. It's clear and simple, it's not unpleasant to the ear if you want to repeat it softly to yourself as you're double-checking your list before reading it out to the greengrocer, and, most importantly, 'pots' is not open to *any* misunderstanding. So I thought!

But I want to tell you a little tale now that might blow your mind. Well, it did mine at the time, although now, if I'm honest I just look back and tut at the stupidity of a certain person, who shall remain nameless – but only for a few more lines.

Let me set the scene. Mary had gone to visit an elderly relative. It was an auntie called Janet and I've mentioned the incident before in a song called 'Poorly Aunt'. Mary thinks the song is rubbish and leaves the room every time I start to play it. But you might like it, readers, so here goes:

Mary, I am missing you, missing you, missing you
Wishing to be kissing you, but, unfortunately, I can't

(Start clapping on the off beat, please, as you carry on with ...)

Mary, I am missing you, missing you, missing you
Wishing to be kissing you, but you're visiting a poorly aunt!

Mmm, I'm not so sure about that song now. Even with the clapping (and I thank those who did put their hands together for the second part), it seems a bit rubbish. Maybe Mary was right. Funny, in't it? At the time I wrote it I was totally convinced of its merits, and remember singing it to a couple called Mr and Mrs Whitticar (she was a lab technician, but I've no idea what he did, I'm afraid…) and I was punching the air as I sang, and they loved it and were clapping along (while Mary just sat on the sofa looking fed up). But, yes, the Whitticars really went mad for that one and I don't know why, because I agree with Mary now – it's really not one of my best ones, and I'm sorry that I forced it on you.

Anyway, with Mary away, I obviously had a lot of housework and domestic duties to undertake. This included a trip to the local greengrocers to purchase a week's supply of fruit and vegetables for a growing family comprising of me, Mary and our young children, Darren and Karen. In Mary's absence, Ken Worthington kindly agreed to accompany me on the family shop. That was good of him, don't you think – considering he's not even in my family! (That's not the bit that might blow your mind – that comes later.)

Ken, being a slightly spindly man, elected to pull Mary's shopping trolley, leaving me to carry a heavy shopping bag (well, it would be heavy on our return trip). But don't feel too sorry for me – I got to enjoy the sound the trolley made on the pavement by walking close to it while stooping slightly with one ear cocked in the direction of the trolley wheels. It was a comforting trundle noise, and it was pleasant to be free for once of the responsibility of having to manoeuvre the trolley which can be quite tricky, as Ken found out on our return from the shops.

I'd already warned Ken about an adverse camber on a section of approaching pavement, but he chose to ignore me. Seconds later I heard the heavily laden trolley swivel on its axis causing Ken to yelp in pain as his wrist was violently wrenched at an awkward angle. More worryingly, several tins of spaghetti hoops (incredibly popular at the time as they were quite a new product, i.e. people weren't negative about them, as they can be now, I notice) had been thrown to the edge of the trolley's main compartment and had to be repositioned in the centre, which took me a while, although Ken recklessly suggested we continue without first checking that the trolley's weight distribution was safe and even.

Note to myself (although feel free to read it too): why on earth am I talking about the journey home? All that concerns us is what happened while we were at the shops. Let's get on to that now, please!

We had just arrived at the greengrocers and, prior to entering the shop, I decided to double-check the shopping list (written by Mary before her departure to visit the poorly aunt). As I was checking it, for some reason Ken asked to see it. I graciously granted his request, thinking nothing of it, but, boy, oh boy, I wish now I'd kept the list to myself.

Ken read the list in silence and then handed it back saying, "Pots? What pots are you buying?" Well, Mary hadn't specified which potatoes, so I told Ken I didn't know. "Whatever's available, Ken," I replied, "Whatever's available will be fine, I'm sure." Well, Ken screwed his face up and became very agitated and started turning red, saying, "That's ridiculous! You should know what type of pots you're looking for. What are the dimensions? Is it a set or separate items you're seeking? Are we talking porcelain or a more basic earthenware? Must they be glazed?"

Can you guess what the misunderstanding was? I'm sure the readers North of the Border will have twigged – and the Welsh readers too in the West, not to mention those Eastern readers lucky enough to live in Mablethorpe or Chapel St Leonards? Even the Southern Softies must have sussed it by now! That's right: Ken Worthington was thinking that 'pots' meant 'pots' as in pots and pans. What a wally!

Sorry it took me a while to get to the point there, readers, but – in my defence – I'm not a professional storyteller, you know. If you want that, then you need to go to the Toby Inn in Millhouses where every second Sunday a lady called Valerie dons a cloak and tells stories to children who are bored of the carvery (how can anyone get bored of a carvery??). Janet Le Roe (a stablemate of mine – like myself she's on the books of Ken Worthington) accompanies Valerie on her acoustic guitar, strumming chords and even doing finger picking when required. That's a skill I've admired ever since I saw Val Doonican do it on the telly and he wasn't even looking down! Mind you, I've got 'fingerpicking humdinger' on my organ – number 59.

Anyway, back to the story. I said, "Why are you being so thick, Ken? Everybody knows that pots means potatoes." Ken replied angrily, "I've never EVER come across that before in my life, John!" Well, it was my turn to get red in the face because I felt that Ken was lying. "You must have!" I hissed angrily, but Ken was adamant that he hadn't.

I don't know who got crosser. Probably Ken, because saliva appeared at the side of his mouth (as in the case of Tony Hatch, when he berated Ken for his dreadful performance on *New Faces* in '73). Then he calmed down a bit and slumped over the shopping trolley, red in the face and close to tears, it seemed to me. The colour slowly drained from his face as he looked at me, almost pleadingly, saying, "John, I've honestly never heard of pots being used as an abbreviation for the word potatoes. I've heard of tatties or spuds, but never pots. Anyway, it's a terrible abbreviation, because it's so open to misinterpretation, don't you see? What happens if you're really ill and a home help needs to do your shopping? If you haven't briefed them properly, they may come back with unwanted kitchenware!" I had no answer to that. Maybe Ken was right, maybe he was wrong. But you know what? Ever since then I've always written the word 'potatoes' on all our shopping lists, just in case!

Whose side were you on in that tatty story, I wonder, dear reader? I do hope mine. It would be helpful if you were, if only so that you could agree with me that Ken Worthington really does… take the biscuit!

Take the Biscuit

I like to take a biscuit
And dunk it in my tea
Hot chocolate – I whisk it
It makes it more frothy
Malibu – I don't risk it
But you know who does? That misfit,
The one who takes the biscuit
Ken Worthington is he!

I like to take a biscuit
A custard cream's my fave
I nibble round the edges
till a diamond shape is made
But a custard cream's not for ever
It's time to have another
And another and another and another...
Four custard creams are never enough
But five is one too many!

I like to take a biscuit
And dunk it in my tea
Hot chocolate – I whisk it
It makes it more frothy
Malibu – I don't risk it
But you know who does? That misfit,
The one who takes the biscuit
Ken Worthington is he!

WITH SPECIAL GUEST **Brian Appleton**

APRIL 2003

1	**GLASGOW** Tron Theatre	0141 552 4267
2	**LEEDS** City Varieties	0113 243 0808
5	**SALFORD QUAYS** The Lowry	0161 876 2000
6	**SHREWSBURY** Music Hall	01743 281 281
7	**WOLVERHAMPTON** Wulfrun Hall	01902 552 121
8	**DERBY** Assembly Rooms	01332 255 800
11	**ISLE OF WIGHT** Quay Arts	01983 528 825
12	**BRIGHTON** Corn Exchange	01273 709 709
13	**BRISTOL** Bierkeller	0117 929 9008/926 8514
14	**EXETER** St George's Hall	01392 211 080/665 866
15	**HARROGATE** Theatre	01423 502 116
16	**DONCASTER** Civic	01302 342 349
17	**HULL** Truck Theatre	01482 323 638
24	**IPSWICH** New Wolsey Theatre	01473 295 900
25	**CARDIFF** Sherman Theatre	02920 646 900
26	**WARWICK** Arts Centre	02476 524 524
27	**OXFORD** Apollo	08706 063 500
30	**NEWARK** Palace Theatre	01636 655 755

MAY 2003

1	**LIVERPOOL** Neptune Theatre	0151 709 7844
2	**STOKE** Victoria Hall	01782 213 800
3	**WAKEFIELD** Opera House	01924 211 311
6	**SCARBOROUGH** Spa Theatre	01723 376 774
7	**MIDDLESBROUGH** Town Hall	01642 242 561
8	**NEWCASTLE** Opera House	0191 232 0899
11	**SHEFFIELD** Crucible	0114 249 6000
12	**BUXTON** Opera House	0845 12 72190
13	**NORWICH** Maddermarket	01603 620 917
14	**TEWKESBURY** Roses Theatre	01684 295 074
15	**WINCHESTER** Theatre Royal	01962 840 440
16	**HEBDEN BRIDGE** Picture House	01422 351 158
18	**NOTTINGHAM** Playhouse	0115 941 9419
21	**CAMBRIDGE** Corn Exchange	01223 357 851
22	**READING** Town Hall	0118 960 6060
23	**LONDON** Shepherds Bush Empire	0870 771 2000
24	**LANCASTER** Dukes Theatre	01524 598 500
25	**PRESTON** Charter Theatre	01772 258 858
26	**LOUTH** Riverhead Theatre	01507 600 350
28	**JERSEY** Opera House	01534 511 115

10. The Man Who Led Llamas

A painter and decorator called Glyn (I'm sorry, I don't know his second name) came to quote recently for redecorating Ken's lounge. I believe Ken's still waiting for the quote, but he's not holding his breath as the chap is extremely busy, and when you hear the next bit you'll understand why. Glyn told Ken he'd fallen off a ladder last year, while painting outside a house at gutter level. He injured himself quite badly, was briefly hospitalised and was so poorly he had a near-death experience. I obviously wouldn't wish that on anyone, but there has been a fortunate repercussion to Glyn's accident: since his recovery Glyn has visited nineteen countries, done a parachute jump from 13,000 feet, abseiled down the side of a medical centre in Dronfield to raise money for ex-military personnel, tried to do hot air ballooning (it was too windy, so he's not completed that challenge yet, although his voucher remains valid until spring 2027, which is good to hear), ridden a quad bike, done paint balling, played crazy golf (now you're talking, Glyn!) and lots of other things he's always dreamed of, including, wait for it… leading llamas round a field!

Oof, blimey! Have you ever heard of that? I imagine that leader of the Lib Dems has done all the others that Glyn's done, but I bet he's not led a llama round a field! It's the latest thing apparently, like axe throwing, which I don't like the sound of at all, but young people are into it, so I've heard, as it's a 'stress buster'. My son Darren and fiancée Jasmin spent an afternoon doing it, in Healey Bottom, I believe, with another young couple whose identity is unknown to me, but they're very nice, apparently. Stop press: Darren and Jasmin have now moved in together into a rented flat. Isn't that great news! Incidentally, Jasmin still works at the leisure centre, although once she played the bugle in the British Army. However, when she left the Armed Forces she was medically downgraded. But Jasmin's not bothered, and I'm delighted to report that her duties at the leisure centre include hiring out squash rackets (a deposit must be left in addition to the hire fee!), and if you lose your swimming trunks, then Jasmin's the lass to go to. "What does your son Darren do then, John?" Well, as I've mentioned many times in the past, Darren is assistant manager at a branch of Bargain Booze. It used to be called Augustus Barnet, which sounds much posher, doesn't it? Ah, well, back to the llamas…

Leading llamas? Round a blinking field? Sounds a bit silly, dun't it, but it's not, according to Glyn. It's a spiritual experience! Glyn told Ken that you get to choose your own llama, you're allowed to put the harness on yourself, then you lead it round the field while immersed in conversation with the llama (if desired, although you may also choose to ignore the llama and walk in silence). And the price? A staggering £60 for one person or £80 for two people for a two-hour session. Poor Glyn was on his tod, so he'd have had to shell out 60 blinking quid just to lead a llama round a field for two hours! What a rip-off. He could have bought a quality power drill from Screwfix for that money, plus a box of drill bits, and probably a step stool with a built-in toolbox, and used the two hours to put a few shelves up (or even box in a boiler?). It's utter madness, in my view. But... talking of madness, 'Leading a Llama' is supposedly very good for your mental health.

Mmm, really? I'm not convinced. If one of those llamas has mental health issues itself, what happens then? Mightn't they be passed on to the person leading them? "Surely that's not going to happen" you may counterclaim. "Llamas are very calm creatures, and that's why they're the ideal animal to help people with psychological problems." I very much doubt that, my friend. Just think about it for a moment… being led round a field every day many times by different strangers (who may be mumbling strange things into your ear), wouldn't that cause severe mental stress in a llama, leading eventually to a total breakdown? Yes, those llamas have probably all gone crackers! They have so many mental health issues of their own that calming down people with psychological problems is just not going to happen – it's a pipe dream…

"Much better, surely," I suggested to Ken, "for Glyn to

have gone to see a horse in a field." Not as exciting perhaps, but it doesn't cost 60 quid. In fact, it's free, and a reliable and therapeutic experience. Usually… hmm, sometimes the blinking horse is hiding behind a big bush and all you can see is their swishing tail, and you feel robbed. It happened to me the other day when I stopped to look at a horse in a field near Killamarsh. The horse saw me – and the moment he did, went and deliberately hid behind a tree. Not a nice thing to do, and for someone battling with their nerves or trying to hang on to their sanity, it could be a life-changing event!

In my case – having currently no mental health issues – the horse's actions just left me a bit cross. I was alone in an icy breeze, shivering by the fence, with only occasional glimpses of his swishing tail, or her tail (it may have been a lady horse – but, if so, it was no lady, in my view!). I had a miserable time waiting for it to come to me, but it never did. I know you shouldn't take things like that personally, but ultimately there's no other way to take them, is there? At the time, I dealt with the rejection by going back to my car and reading through old MOT certificates and the vehicle's service history (yes, all the way back to 1981 – it is a Y Reg, after all!) while sucking a Murray Mint, which did cheer me up to some degree.

"Has Glyn visited Keswick Pencil Museum?" I asked Ken. If he's trying to cram it all in and do the most exciting things he can in a short period, then surely the Pencil Museum should be on the list. Ken said that it wasn't a place Glyn had mentioned. I'm staggered by that. This chap is probably planning a trip to 'Country Number 20' as we speak, but instead he'd be much better off filling his flask with oxtail soup and heading to the Lake District to visit the Pencil Museum where – let's not forget – you get to stand next to the tallest pencil in the world.

(Please note: if you ever feel a bit big-headed, it's humbling to realise that you're actually smaller than a pencil, so why not try it yourself some time?)

I said to Ken: "He may have visited nineteen countries – this Glyn bloke – and he may have led a mad llama around a field, but has he been to the Heights of Abraham near Matlock or the Crich Tramway Village in, erm... Crich? Has he even visited Mother Shipton's Cave near Knaresborough?" Mind you, I never have. We were going to go, but Mary didn't like the idea of spending Sunday afternoon in a damp cave, and who can blame her? My concerns included the fear that Mother Shipton might not have been there in person and then – like the hiding horse – you'd have felt, well, this is all a bit of a swizz!

We wish Glyn the best of luck with fulfilling his bucket list and hope that on it is 'Decorate Ken Worthington's lounge'! Yes, please, Glyn – when you're ready, young man, Ken is waiting! Let's close with a song which I've sent a cassette of to Glyn (via Ken and with Dolby on, of course, so it's not too hissy). Having had a near-death experience, this song will surely speak loud and clear to the man who led a llama, and you too, I hope..

Rapidly Downhill

Childhood was unpleasant
Everything went too slow
Always living in the present
Waiting for bones to grow

Then came adolescence
Not a nice stage to be in
Learning life's hard lessons
With acne upon my chin

Marriage made me middle-aged
Soon I'll be an OAP
But then how happy I will be

Going...

Rapidly downhill
Rapidly downhill
The view's enticing, life's exciting,
Even though I'm gravely ill

Rapidly downhill
Rapidly downhill
Like skiing in snow, what a way to go
Hurry up and write your will

Being fit and healthy made
My life one long chore
Open this jar of marmalade
Put away that ironing board

Sanding, drilling, Polyfilling
Perched on windowsills
DIY, PAYE
Juggling household bills

Soon I'll be an old man
And as ill health kicks in
You'll see my frown turn into a grin

As I go rapidly downhill
Rapidly downhill
The view's enticing, life's exciting,
Even though I'm gravely ill

Rapidly downhill
Rapidly downhill
Like skiing in snow, what a way to go
Hurry up and write your will!

11. Confusion in the Co-op

I was in our local Co-op recently, and as I shopped I realised they were playing a song by Simply Red, one of Mary's favourite bands, and – let's be honest – they're everyone's favourite band really, aren't they? Put it another way: I don't think anyone could ever say anything negative about Simply Red. And if they did, they'd be swiftly pounced on by everyone else. In the past, perhaps you could have teased the singer Mick Hucknall for being a 'ginge', but that's illegal now, in't it? Having said that, I'm about to commit the cardinal sin and do just that – criticise Simply Red for a line in one of their songs. It's a line I heard that day in the Co-op, or – to be more accurate – didn't hear! I urgently need to discuss this, with Mick ideally, but as I haven't got his contact details I'll have to run it by you, dear reader. I do hope you can help me…

I was in the Co-op, as I've stated several times now (let's hope everyone knows where I was that day!) and I was looking for the green 'pestio' in readiness for a visit by my daughter Karen. She loves that pestio, you see, although it looks like mould in a jar (and let's be honest, the red variety looks like it's bits of rusty metal in a jar!). Karen lives near Hebden Bridge, West Yorkshire, with her friend Maxine, I mean, erm. . . Morag (the veterinary nurse who I hope and pray doesn't make the switch to professional witch). Karen is currently in between jobs. She was a nursery nurse when she lived in Mansfield, but now she wants to retrain to be... a bus driver! So she told Mary recently. Blimey, watch this space! They've just got themselves a rescue dog, which I question the wisdom of as it's tying both ladies down, in't it? Neither Karen nor Morag are courting currently and caring for a dog isn't going to leave them much time for dating and finding Mr Right. I want to be a grandad before too long, you know, and so does Mary. Well, a grandma. Perhaps we'll need to rely on Darren and Jasmin for that…

Anyway, I was in the Co-op (as you know!), concentrating hard on locating the pestio (or pesto, as most people foolishly like to call it, so I suppose I should too. It's just that 'pestio' sounds better to me. Like 'cafetiary' – much better to my ears than 'cafetière'). Pestio hides itself well among all the more brightly coloured sauces and pickles, have you noticed? So it's incredibly difficult to locate on the shelves in supermarkets. Mind you, not as hard as finding crab paste in the little jars. Those jars get pushed to the back now, and it's not fair as older people sometimes give up looking for it and have to go without. I know they've got triple lock and all that, so they can probably afford to buy fresh crab and posh thin sliced salmon, but that's not the point. Besides, elderly folk prefer the taste and texture of crab paste and salmon paste and – my goodness – so do I!

I was so intent on finding that blinking pestio, I'm amazed my brain even registered the sumptuous tones of Mick H. singing one of the Simply Red classics. But it did, and gradually I relaxed and stopped worrying so much about searching for a jar of mould. 'Stars', I believe the song is called. The lyrics are extremely clever and contain brilliant imagery and wordplay, as we've come to expect from the impish redhead. (I think I'm alright to call him that, am I?) Anyway, I noticed everyone was nodding as they shopped, with a slight smile on their faces, and who can blame them? Like me, most folk were no longer concentrating on doing their shopping but rather on appreciating the beautiful music we were hearing, not to mention Mick's deep meaningful lyrics, which are so universal in their appeal even a toddler could relate to them. That line about wanting to fall from the stars into your arms is my favourite. Although it wouldn't be a good idea to actually do that as you'd be travelling way too fast and would hurt somebody, including yourself, but I'm confident Mick knows that. If he doesn't know that, then somebody should tell him! Someone mild-mannered like Professor Brian Cox could explain it to Mick in a way that wouldn't cause Mick offence or make him look foolish. Although when you're as cool as Mick, I doubt if looking foolish is ever an issue.

And the line about loving the thought of coming home

to you, that's another gorgeous one from the gifted pen of Mr Hucknall (It's fine to call him Mr Hucknall, surely? That's his name, after all!). It's a line from a song called 'Fairground', I believe. It's a shame that song wasn't played in the Co-op that day as well, because there was time for me to hear it – I still hadn't located the pestio – and I would have been able to relate to it. You see, I was 'loving the thought' of returning home to my wife Mary with the pestio, if I ever eventually found it. Well, where else would I have been going? The recycling centre? No, not that day – I didn't have my trailer attached to my Austin Ambassador (Y Reg). Anyhow, with that line, Mick cleverly taps into the psyche of the nation, because we *all* love the thought of coming home to our loved ones. With that line Mick is entering the hallowed territory of Chris Rea and his driving home for Christmas song, would you not say, readers? The thing about the driver next to him being just the same? Of course, he is. We're all knights of the road together. Fantastic! However, I don't like the line "Top to toe in tailbacks." It's an unpleasant reminder of how congested the roads can get over the Yuletide period, and I'd have preferred it if Chris could have kept quiet about that! It's that line that perhaps prevents the song from being an all-time classic. Ah, well, never mind, Chris, it's still a cracking number!

Back to Mick Hucknall and the gorgeous song I heard in the Co-op. Unfortunately, there's one line in the chorus of 'Stars' that I just don't understand because I can't hear what the lad's singing. It's in the second part of the chorus, after he's repeated the line about falling straight into somebody's arms. In the next line he mumbles something unintelligible in a really high register, and then he sings "I hope you comprehend". Well, no, I *don't* comprehend, Mick, and I can't believe anybody understands what you're singing there. And presumably that's why you're asking the question, because you know we didn't clock what you sang in the bit before. You're hoping that we did, but I'm sorry, we blinking well didn't, and we certainly *don't comprehend*!

In a way, I suppose it's thoughtful of Mick Hucknall to sing that – it shows he's aware of the problem and is flagging it up. But, Michael, I'd have preferred it if you'd just sang the words a bit more clearly and in a lower register. It's so frustrating not being able to comprehend the line. Oof, I've just suddenly thought – maybe the reason we don't comprehend what he's singing there is because it's sung so high he's going out of human audio range? What do you think, readers? It's possible, in't it? I remember I used to struggle to understand some of the lines in Rubettes numbers. That lad with the beret – his voice was ridiculously high – 'Sugar Baby Love'. Oof, piercing. Mind you, they've gone a bit quiet now, the Rubettes. Oof, maybe it's because they sang higher and higher until they went out of audio range? Perhaps they're still around, but we just can't hear them! Don't worry, that was just a joke. (Note: you won't find many jokes in this book, as they tend to waste time, but occasionally I'll slip one in, like I did just then. And I hope you agree – it was worth it!) But, yes, of course the Rubettes are still around – ploughing the club circuit along with Showaddywaddy and Black Lace. Good on yer, lads. Hope you have a cracking night and see you on the other side!

Maybe I should ask Mary what Mick is singing there? Mary might know as she's a big Simply Red fan, and she's just had her ears syringed at Specsavers. Or Brian Cox – perhaps he'd be able to work it out? He's a very clever man (although he can seem a bit dopey and his lips are a little on the moist side, have you noticed?). But I suspect Prof Bri (as I like to call him – well, I just did then!) can comprehend anything. My guess is he'll even know when Comet Hale-Bopp's coming back. Do you remember that one? A good twenty years ago, wasn't it, when it graced our night skies? I miss it, don't you? Mind you, it could play havoc with your navigation if you were out at night on Britain's roads. If you don't remember the Hale-Bopp comet, let me remind you now with a rendition of my slightly spooky rock ballad all about it.

Blatherwyke

I was on the M1
Stuck in heavy traffic
I'd had enough of it
And decided to get off it
Cruising down a country lane
The wind upon my bonnet
I saw a sign for Blatherwyke
A name which invites comment

There is a place called Blatherwyke
You might not have heard of it
But half a mile down to the right
And I'd have come across it
But I was lost and it was late
I needed to step on it
And the tail of the Hale-Bopp comet
Was guiding me away from it

Soon I was on the A1
Heading north for Newark
Though my progress was hampered
By road works at Stamford
Home was getting closer
And I was keen to view it
Keen, too, to view Blatherwyke
Well, I had my chance and blew it

I could have gone to Blatherwyke
So why didn't I do it?
Half a mile down to the right
And I'd have passed right through it
But to be fair, I don't live there
There was no reason to have done it
And the tail of the Hale-Bopp comet
Was guiding me away from it
Yes, the tail of the Hale-Bopp comet
Was guiding me away
Oh, maybe some day
I'll get on my bike
And visit Blatherwyke...

12.
The Ballad of Dangly Man

CAST YOUR MIND BACK TO A FINE NIGHT IN MAY.
SPIRITS WERE HIGH AS I STARTED TO PLAY...

LUCKILY EDALE MOUNTAIN RESCUE APPEARED ON THE SCENE AND THE AUDIENCE CRIED 'PHEW!'

CKETS
THE MORAL IS PLAIN AS THE DERBYSHIRE MOORS:
WHEN YOU COME TO MY SHOWS PLEASE COME THROUGH THE DOORS.

NOT OVER CLIFFS DISTURBING JACKDAWS... AND IF YOU BLAME YOUR SATNAV, YOU'LL BE CLUTCHING AT STRAWS.

SOME DIDN'T BELIEVE IT,
SOME CALLED IT A FARCE.
IT COULD ONLY HAVE HAPPENED
IN THE DEVIL'S ARSE.

BUT WE'LL ALWAYS REMEMBER THAT NIGHT, AND BE HAPPY DANGLY MAN WAS RESCUED IN A GIANT NAPPY!

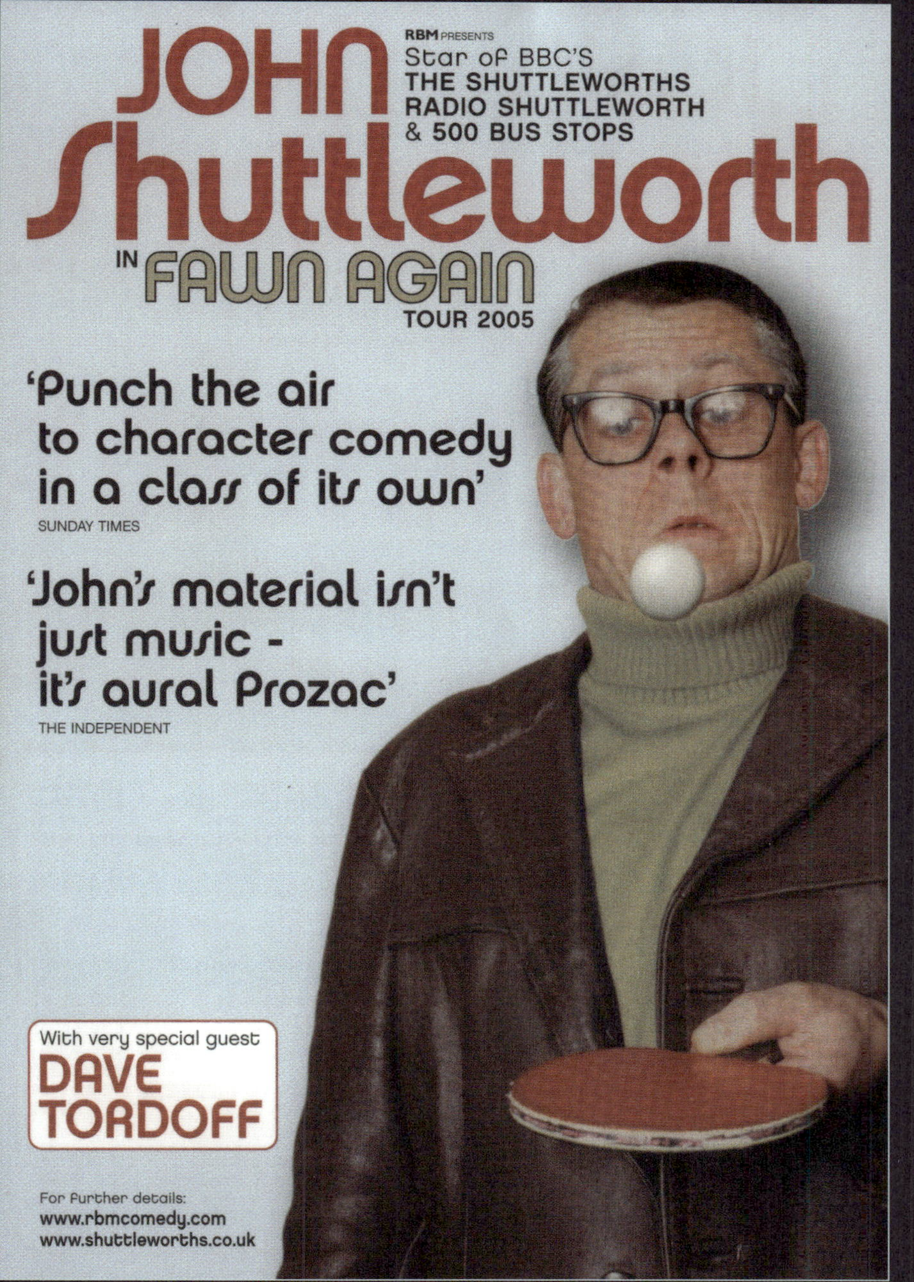

IN **FAWN AGAIN**

TOUR 2005

'Punch the air to character comedy in a class of its own'

SUNDAY TIMES

'John's material isn't just music - it's aural Prozac'

THE INDEPENDENT

With very special guest

DAVE TORDOFF

For further details:

www.rbmcomedy.com

www.shuttleworths.co.uk

13. Flare Affair

Ken Worthington once told me that when he was a teenager his mother bought him a pair of flared jeans – or 'bell bottoms' I believe they were called back then. It was the late sixties, and Ken was twelve or thirteen and trying to be a hippy, or even a beatnik, I think he said. I don't really know what a beatnik is, but it doesn't sound very savoury, does it? Anyhow, the Worthington family weren't rich, so these flares were secondhand, and sadly they were far too long for Ken. He soon realised he wouldn't be able to wear them without the length of the leg being drastically reduced. (Interestingly enough, the waist was bang on for little Ken, and required no alteration, and this must be because he had quite a podgy tummy at the time.)

So, that evening Ken's mother got out her sewing basket to take up the flares, and presumably Ken had to stand stock-still while his mum stuck pins in his ankle area. Now this would've required a lot of trust by Ken, don't you think, that he wasn't going to get pricked by the pins? But come on – it was Ken's mother, and if you can't trust your own mother, who can you trust? Hang on, what if there had been a breakdown of trust between Ken and his mother due to childhood neglect or mistreatment (including poor weaning techniques)? I'm not insinuating there were any trust issues, but if there were, it would explain Ken's occasional erratic behaviour, plus the nightly visitations by a hooded axe man at the end of his bed (oof, imagine that – well, no, don't – it's horrible!). It might even explain the funny face Ken made to the camera while competing on *New Faces* in '73.

I should add at this stage that Ken – who, as you know, is a small man – was an even smaller teenager. Let's put it this way – his inside leg measurement was not a high number. "Was it in single figures?" I hear you enquire. No, don't be ridiculous. Even Ernie Wise's inside leg measurement would have been in double figures, but Ken's may have been in the lower twenties...? To cut a long story short… Oof, I've just made a little joke there, I realise, did you spot that (because this story's all about cutting a long trouser short!)? Anyway, Ken's mother had to trim the trousers from the bottom, obviously, and, erm, well… some of you may have already guessed what happened. By the time his mother had adjusted the trousers to the correct length, the flare that Ken was so desperate to have in his new trousers (so he could look like a beatnik) was completely lost. Essentially, Ken's flares were now drainpipes, like what a mod would wear – a look and a style Ken was trying to get away from! Can you imagine poor Ken's disappointment? (I've adapted an existing song to try to help you imagine it.)

Poor Ken, poor Ken
The flare in his jeans was only to-ken
Poor Ken, poor Ken
His spirit had been bro-ken

But Ken was a fighter and the plucky lad refused to give up on his dream of owning flared jeans. So, next day he requested that his mother insert a triangular section of cloth into each trouser leg to recreate the flare that had been lost during the trimming. You'd think she'd have been able to use some of the jean material left over after she'd shortened Ken's jeans. But the foolish lady had given it to the rag-and-bone man that very morning, so the only cloth available for this was from the hem of the lounge curtains which were made from a heavy orange velour. As you can imagine, it looked awful, and the inserted flare sections were heavy and flopped to the side in a most unfortunate way. Ken was too embarrassed to wear them for the school dance, and can you blame him? Ken told me he only ever wore those flares once (to please his mother) on a walk with a neighbour's sausage dog round the block one night when it was extremely dark. (Notice Ken didn't even have his own dog to offer him solace in his hour of need?) What a sad story – unless you're a bit of a sicko who enjoys laughing at other people's distress.

And if that's you, you'll probably revel in what happened to Ken after he came last on *New Faces* in '73. As I've already stated, his wife Rhiannon left him and took up with a builder called Martin in Stoney Middleton.

Despite moving out, Rhiannon decided she should keep the marital home (as she needed a lot of storage for her collection of harps – she accompanied Ken on *New Faces*, of course, playing the harp while Ken tootled on his clarinet and did a tap dance), and so poor Ken was forced to go and live in a caravan on the banks of a canal in the Dronfield Woodhouse area. Down on his luck and broken-hearted, one night Ken made himself a last supper using the few items he had left in the caravan larder. These included lentils, instant mash, anchovies, tinned peaches and a bottle of Henderson's Relish that was four years out of date. He put all the items in a big pan and heated it up and then ate the resultant stew.

I've always been of the belief that Ken's stew was really nourishing and made him feel on top of the world, and some readers may have heard me mention this before and been of the same view. But, oof… I got my facts wrong. Sincere apologies if you've previously heard me praising the meal. I've since learnt from Ken that the meal tasted disgusting and made him quite ill. In fact, that night he spent several hours on his porta potty. Next morning, Ken was so depressed (because of Rhiannon leaving him, losing his home to lots of harps, plus the final straw of having a chronic tummy upset) that he considered taking his own life. As he was already next to the canal, he decided it made sense to end it all by throwing himself into the water. But Ken made the mistake of testing the temperature first and, well... it was just too cold for him. The shock of the water temperature brought him to his senses and he abandoned his suicide bid. Thank goodness – and besides, he still had a bad tummy, and, as any health professional will tell you, you should *never ever* go in the water when you've digestive problems!

What a nana Ken is, eh? He really does take the biscuit, I think you'll agree. And although he's been my next-door neighbour and sole agent for, oof, forty years or so, I still wonder if I really know the man. This does beg the musical question:

Can You Ken Ken?

You're like a halo
You go above some people's heads
You're like a biro
Sometimes you're blue
And sometimes red

You're like a Volvo
You keep your lights on in the day
Like a last Rolo
You rarely give yourself away

Can you ken Ken?
Can you ken Ken?
You may be able to can can
But can you ken Ken?

You're like a Polo
Your hole is greater than your parts
But you're not like Eric Bristow
I.e. you're terrible at darts

("Very amusing, but what am I really like, John?" Well, Ken, since you ask...)

You're like you
You're like you

And no other comparison will do
You're like you
You're like you
Not quite, but close enough for you to sue!

Can you ken Ken?
Can you ken Ken?
You may be able to can can
But can you ken Ken..?

(Because I know I can't!)

14. Brian May Is a Water Rat

I didn't believe it when I first heard the words "Brian May is a water rat". Somebody just said it to me one day. I think it was an ex-colleague of Ken Worthington's called Dale, erm, something… who had worked extensively for the Variety Club of Great Britain. As you may know (you probably do as I've mentioned it many times in the past), I once helped raise money to take poorly children to Disney World in Florida. I performed Men at Work's 'Do You Come From The Land Down Under?' at a charity garden party in Nether Edge. I banged my tooth on the microphone grille during that bit about the Vegemite sandwich – you know the bit – and chipped my tooth. But please don't blame Men at Work – as tempting as that may be. It was completely my own fault. I got a bit cocky, you see, and got too close to the microphone. To make matters worse, we didn't raise enough money, so we had to take the poorly youngsters to the Abbeydale Industrial Hamlet. But I drove the minibus – fantastic!

Before I tell you more about Brian May and the shock

revelation that he was a water rat, I'd love to just tell you about another occasion I drove the minibus. Is that okay? It's just that I've never mentioned it before, and I think it's high time I did. It was a day trip to Riber Castle a good few years ago with some disadvantaged youngsters. (I don't think they were poorly, this lot, just disadvantaged.) Anyway, Ken Worthington came along and after the trip he told me that Ken Dodd's niece had been on the trip. Yes, that's right – Ken Dodd's niece! But silly Ken Worthington told me too late. By the time I found out, everyone had disembarked from the minibus and gone home, so there was no way to identify the niece, take her to one side and probe her (calmly but insistently) to verify the claim. I imagine she'd have had crazy hair, slightly bucked teeth and a squinty-eyed look as did the great man, but I don't remember seeing anyone on the minibus who fitted that description. So was Ken imagining things? Or did he make the story up? I wouldn't put it past him. If so, it's another fine example of him 'taking the biscuit'! Anyway, we're in grave danger of straying from the story about Brian May.

And what a story it is! When I first heard the words "Brian May is a water rat" I was chilled to the core. Brian May? A rat? And he lives in the water? And then I suddenly remembered that being a water rat is a good thing. It doesn't mean a love rat or even a real water rat. It means that you're a sort of Freemason and you like to raise money to help people less fortunate than yourself. And let's be honest, most people are less fortunate than

Brian May (the famous rock guitarist from Queen, in case you didn't know), so he must be incredibly busy as a water rat. It must be a full-time occupation, so how can he spare any time to talk to his wife, actress Anita Dobson (Angie Watts in long-running soap *EastEnders*), let alone do jobs about the house?

It's funny because Brian May always gives the impression of being quite calm. How can he be? He's been on the Queen's roof! If ever I meet Brian, I won't be asking him what it's like being on the road with Queen – I'll be asking him what it's like being on the roof of the Queen! (I might also ask him if Anita makes him get down the washing basket. I suspect she does, and so he should, as Brian is rather tall and gangly – the perfect physique to be the 'washing basket getter-downerer!') Oof, that's a strange phrase, which I'm not sure I'll be using again.

Yes, I would quiz Brian about the state of the guttering and the lead flashings on the Queen's roof. (I presume they're lead and not a cheap substitute material from Wickes.) And yet, hang on – would Brian have had time to take that information in? He had to play 'Happy Birthday' on his guitar, remember? He played it faultlessly, as I recall. Obviously you'd expect him to, being an experienced guitar player. Still, the nerves would've been there. And it's not that easy a tune to play, you know? I'm just going to attempt it now on my organ to demonstrate how hard it is – it's that bit where it jumps really high that gets me. 'Happy BIRTHday, dear Queenie!' Yeah, I just played one wrong note there this time – that's not too bad for me. I normally do two or three wrong notes in that section. But Brian was impeccable throughout. And all the while he played I remember the breeze was lightly ruffling his long mane of lustrous well-maintained hair.

I'm going to shock a few people now, but I place Brian's guitar playing on a par with Chris Rea's. Maybe Brian is even a tiny bit better, but Chris, in my view, has the edge because he possesses a gravelly voice with a Geordie twang, whereas Brian May is softly spoken (with no twang). Chris used that gravelly voice to massive effect on 'Driving Home For Christmas', which, as I've already stated, is my favourite Christmas song of all time. I suspect it's everybody's, if they're honest with themselves. But, sadly, some people aren't capable of being honest, and it's a shame. I'd quite like to meet up socially with Chris Rea, and indeed Brian May, and Anita Dobson too, of course. And I tell you what – Ken Dodd's niece would be more than welcome to join us. If there *is* such a person... Hmm, I'm beginning to have me doubts. Come on, love, don't be shy. If Ken wasn't mistaken and you really are a relation of Doddy's, come forward and say hello!

One gentleman I did meet up with socially – for half an hour in a music museum in Coventry in 2017 – is crooner Vince Hill. He was a lovely man, but was he a Water Rat, I wonder? I forgot to ask him and it's too late now as, sadly, Vince passed on in 2023. He's now hanging out with Doddy and Brucie and all the other deceased stars up there in Showbiz Heaven. But for a few years while Vince Hill was still alive – and before I met him in 2017, obviously –

I was curious as to his whereabouts (as he'd gone a bit quiet), so I wrote this reggae-based number, which music scholars might argue recalls the work of Aswad. Oof, they've gone a bit quiet an' all. Whatever happened to them – not to mention Ken Dodd's niece? Oof, there's far too many questions that require answers. Let's just try to answer this question for now, shall we?

Whatever Happened to Vince Hill?

Whatever happened to Vince Hill
Last seen on *Pebble Mill*?
In beige safari suit with butterscotch tan
What a star! Oh, what a man!

Whatever happened to *Pebble Mill*?
I never got my fill.
A Royal Marine parachutes into the crowd
To be greeted by host, Donny MacLeod

Whatever happened to Donny MacLeod?
He never seems to be around
(Oof, there's a good reason for that...)
He died in '84 aged 52
He died as everyone of us is condemned to do

And what will happen to Vince Hill
When he passes away as one day he surely will?
Please don't die, Vince. Do something clever
Be the first light entertainer to live for ever and
ever!

And I will weep when Vince has gone
And put 'Edelweiss' on
It reached number two in the charts, didn't quite
make number one
And one – of course – is the time *Pebble Mill* was
on!

15.
The Last Time I Lost My Temper

My wife Mary might disagree here, but I'm sure it was in 2011 when I last lost my temper. One morning, my son Darren opened a packet of Weetabix the wrong way round, and I just couldn't believe he'd done such a crazy thing. Furious with the lad, I snatched the packet off him and demanded that he go and fetch the Sellotape from the kitchen drawer. But he couldn't find it, which increased my anger still further. I went and found the Sellotape myself and sealed up the end of the Weetabix box that had been opened in error. Then I turned the box the right way up and opened the packet correctly. But because I was so angry, I accidentally ripped the cardboard tab – you know, the little flap that slips into the narrow slit which closes the cereal packet (immediately after use, please!).

Yep, I tore the tab, and so of course I needed the Sellotape again. But because I was angry, my hand-to-eye coordination was poor. To make matters worse, there was a tiny mating surface for the Sellotape to cling to, so the repair job took me blinking ages. It sounds like I'm making excuses, but these are the realities of the situation which you should know about to assist you in understanding why I was so angry. As I conducted the repair, I kept noticing Darren's eyes glazing over and his mouth falling open and then shutting again as if he was nodding off, so that was another thing making me cross. (He should have been wide awake watching what I was doing so he could learn how to repair a cereal packet for when he became a father himself!) So, yes, readers, I was, to put it mildly – hopping mad!

I've just thought: it's a good job that *The Repair Shop* wasn't on TV back then, because if those lads who do those amazing repairs on vintage toys had seen me struggling, they'd have had a right laugh, I'm sure. Or would they? Hmm… well, I reckon they're sensitive to people's emotions and they'd have clocked my distress and taken pity on me. They'd have taken the Weetabix box off me (slowly and gently, you know, they wouldn't have snatched it off me – that would have risked further damage to the cardboard!) and they'd have spent a lot of time making the torn tab as good as new. And they'd have made a seamless repair on the end opened in error an' all. They wouldn't have needed to, but they'd have done it anyway, because they're perfectionists. I suspect one of them might even have taken it home and worked on the repairs through the night, 'cause they do that sometimes, don't they, with difficult jobs?

And then when the Weetabix box was finally handed back to me, with my son Darren by my side, wide awake and smiling gratefully, the emotions would have flowed. That one with the bushy beard, I reckon he'd have been appointed to do the repair and he'd get a bit misty-eyed as I thanked him. And the tears would well up in my eyes too, because, let's face it, after all that anger and negative emotion I'd experienced, having someone do such a perfect repair on your cereal box *would* get you choked up. Sadly, it didn't happen, because *The Repair Shop* wasn't gracing our screens back then, but it's a nice fantasy I can dwell on in low moments. In reality, what did happen? Well, an hour later, when I had a fully functional Weetabix box once more, I was feeling… not cock-a-hoop but not too bad, especially after Darren and I had both eaten a nice big bowl of Weetabix and Darren had finally said, "Sorry, Dad, I'll try and be more careful next time." Kids, eh?

I don't know about you, but that's made me want to go straight to the cupboard and get meself a big bowl of cereal! But, instead, I'm going to be sensible and have a sweetie instead. I'll just nip to my Y Reg sitting under my carport, open the glove compartment where I know there's a packet of cherry drops, and remove one sweetie. (I'll also have to remove the wrapper before popping it in my mouth as they are individually wrapped, of course.) Erm, to be honest, I'm experiencing a little heartburn – as I often do mid-morning – and I'd have preferred a cooling mint. Oo, I suddenly remember the excitement of having my first Polo Mint – do you?

My First Polo

I remember my first Polo – do you?
The glint of silver paper
As my father said – here, take a
Sweetie that will make you feel brand new

I remember my first Polo – do you?
Trembling, I held the Polo,
Surprised to see a hole, though
Sensing what it was about to do

It gave my tongue activity
As the mint's flavours bored into me
Turning my grey world azure blue
Sucking it was cathartic
I was suddenly in the Arctic
As through my young lungs a cold wind blew

I remember my first Polo – do you?
If you think I mean a car, though,
You're very wide of the mark, oh
There lies a 'Golf' between our points of view

(Note: That's a rather clever pun, I hope you agree, readers!)

It gave my tongue activity
As the mint's flavours bored into me

Turning my grey world azure blue
Sucking it was cathartic
I was suddenly in the Arctic
Thank goodness I was carsick
That's why my father introduced me to
The Polo - as opposed to the Rolo

(which might have been a bit rich for my tummy)

I remember my first Polo – do you?

16. James Martin and the Outrageously-Priced Chopping Board

I feel awful saying this, but I've completely lost interest in wanting to meet up socially with TV quiz show presenter Bradley Walsh. The thing is – he's clearly too busy to reply to any of my letters. And he obviously didn't like the audio cassette collection *Ballads For Bradley* that I'd lovingly compiled. I took great care to ensure the Dolby button was engaged so the recordings wouldn't be too hissy for him. I made a special cassette cover from shiny coloured paper and bought a brand-new Jiffy bag (to house the audio cassette) from the post office. I even posted it first class, enclosing a signed photo with a personalised inscription, 'Howdy, cheeky fella!' That was Ken's suggestion. I thought it was a bit odd, but he insisted Bradley would like it. Mmm, I'm not so sure he wouldn't have preferred 'To Mr Walsh and family, warmest wishes from Mr Shuttleworth and family'. But, anyway, the deed is done, I've yet to hear back from him, and it's been over two years now, so – as I've already stated – I don't really care any more.

In Bradley's defence, he may have a valid excuse for not getting back to me and accepting my invitation to an afternoon in our home (to include a welcome soft drink and one cooked meal). Bradley must be incredibly busy – co-hosting *Gladiators* with his son Barney, as well as continuing to present the ever popular TV quiz show *The Chase*, not to mention doing personal appearances, plus he may have an ongoing DIY project at home that his wife's insisting he finish. So – and here's the curious thing – even if he found a spare few hours to hang out with yours truly, with all that going on, would I actually want to hang out with him?

You see, if Bradley Walsh ever did decide to come a-calling, I know he'd be stringing me along throughout the whole visit, pretending he was interested in meeting me and Mary and looking round my home. But the reality is this: he wouldn't have time to study my work bench or examine my power tools or have a little play with Kirsty our Scottie dog (oof, sorry – Westie dog!), let alone have a knock up at ping pong. (Notice I didn't say "best out of three". I know that even a whole game would be out of the question!) No disrespect to the great man, but Bradley would constantly be checking his watch, then apologising for doing so. His driver waiting outside would keep calling his mobile to say, "Are you done, Mr Walsh? We really should be leaving to get to the TV studio!" And I'd have to raise my hands in a conciliatory fashion and say, "It's fine, Bradley. Don't worry about it. Yes, Mary has cooked you a lovely shepherd's pie, but it doesn't matter. Just go, please!" But inside I'd be resenting him for having to go, and Bradley would pick up on that and feel bad himself, so, you know, things would get way too fraught, so let's just forget it…

I'm not the least bit downhearted because now my earnest wish is to meet up socially with (besides Brian May, Ken Dodd's niece, etc) guess who? Well, I bet you can't guess, so I'll have to tell you. TV chef James Martin, that's who! "Erm… James Martin?" Some of you may be wondering, "Who the heck is that?" Oh, you might not recognise the name, but you'll have seen him on the telly. He's on all the time, especially at the weekend. Always got a big knife in his hand and his head down as he conducts interviews with celebs who sit on the other side of the studio in high chairs (not chairs for a baby, I don't mean that. Unless he's interviewing a baby, and he hasn't done that yet, as far as I'm aware. But, hmm, he'd be very good at that, I'm sure). Yes, I'd say James Martin is one of the nation's favourite chefs. Not as instantly recognisable perhaps as the effervescent Ainsley Harriot, or the deeply troubled Gordon Ramsay. But he is one of my heroes. After all, it can't be easy to do interviews with your head down while you're chopping vegetables, but James manages it with aplomb. In fact, I'd go so far as to say he's the finest exponent of this special skill currently operating in the UK!

There are some very interesting facts about James that you might not know. For instance, he is an Honorary Professor of the University of West London School of Hospitality and Tourism. You can't make stuff like that up, can you? And I didn't, I promise – it's totally true. As is the fact that recently James won Personality of the Year for the second time at the Fortnum & Mason Food and Drink Awards 2021. Hang on… 2021 isn't that recent. Did he win the award in 2022 for the third time? And what about 2023 and 2024? There's no mention of that online (I've been looking this up on Mary's tablet, you see). Hmm… suddenly James's wonderful accolades don't seem quite so impressive. And when you add this next shock fact into the mix, you start to wonder if James is actually the shining star we all think he is. I'm talking about his own brand of chopping board which sells on his website for a staggering £180 and yet which – by his own admission – "might split over time". That's unbelievable! And James seems to have no shame about it when he declares: "Some cracking and movement will undoubtedly occur over time but hopefully this will add to the enjoyment of your piece".

Is he having a laugh? No, it won't add to my enjoyment, my friend. I'll be sending it back and demanding a full refund! Well, I won't actually, because I won't be buying one in the first place! Bit cheeky asking that kind of money, don't you think, readers, when you can buy a large chopping board (with non-slip feet and a deep drip juice groove) that won't split – 'cause it's made from plastic – for £3.99 from our DIY shop. £180?! I've been offered less for my Austin Ambassador Y Reg! Don't worry, I didn't take it – although I was mildly tempted, as the brakes were playing up and at the time the glove compartment door was sticking. Interestingly, James also does rolling pins for £35. Hmm… slightly better value, and I suppose I could just about afford one of those as a gift for Mary, who is a big James Martin fan. But why would I when they only cost three quid at the Pound Shop? Still, it might be worth developing a friendship with James, as it could lead to receiving those items as free gifts. Crafty, eh? Yes, well, you don't get something for nothing these days, do you? And I'd be more than happy to send James a tape of my song demos in exchange. Perhaps they should be 'food-related' songs, of which I have written plenty over the years. Here's one now which was written to a slow bluesy beat. I'm sorry about that – blues is a bit sleazy, in't it, but it seems to work for this number, which is all about the problems of eating when you're a bit depressed.

Heartache and Heartburn

I've got heartache and heartburn
I belch between sobs
Heartache and heartburn
I belch between sobs
When I visit the pantry
I'm holding my hanky

Since my baby left me
(The ultimate snub)
I've had heartache and heartburn
I find solace in grub
Some go to the pub, Lord,
I go to the cupboard
Or the fridge. Take me to the fridge, I mean the bridge!

Since my love has gone
I'm on the Gaviscon
My pain is made easier
By Milk of Magnesia
And if I don't have any,
I reach for a Rennie

I've got heartache and heartburn
I belch between sobs

Heartache and heartburn
I belch between sobs
Why did she refuse me?
Pardon, excuse me!

17. Peeping Peter

ONE EVENING, AS I WAS PAINTING MY BEDROOM CEILING, I HEARD SOMEONE AT THE FRONT GATE.

IT WAS JOAN CHITTY WHO HAD ARRANGED TO ATTEND A LOCAL EXERCISE CLASS WITH MY WIFE MARY.

I INVITED JOAN TO ASSESS THE ACTION OF OUR GARDEN GATE WHICH - AFTER A RECENT OILING - I FELT WAS MUCH IMPROVED.

JOAN READILY AGREED IT WAS!

MARY JOINED ME AT THE WINDOW, INFORMING JOAN SHE WOULDN'T BE MUCH LONGER.

MARY SUGGESTED THAT AFTER PAINTING THE CEILING, I MIGHT LIKE TO PAINT THE WINDOW FRAME?

MEANWHILE, NEXT-DOOR NEIGHBOUR AND SOLE AGENT KEN WORTHINGTON WAS HARD AT WORK...
...SECURING ME A MUSICAL BOOKING AT A LOCAL REST HOME.

KEN TELEPHONED ME WITH THE DETAILS: A NOSTALGIC SING-ALONG IN LITTLE LONGSTONE...
...THE VERY NEXT DAY!

JOAN - STILL WAITING FOR MARY - JOINED KEN IN ADMIRING HIS NEW PURCHASE!

Smugglers

OH NO... I HAD FORGOTTEN! AND THERE WAS LITTLE TIME IN WHICH TO PURCHASE MY OWN PRESENT FOR MARY!

WHEN SHE ARRIVED HOME
FROM STEPCLASS AND SAW
JOAN'S HANDIWORK...

...MARY WAS NOT
BEST PLEASED!

THE NEXT DAY, AS KEN AND I DROVE TO THE ENGAGEMENT AT THE REST HOME IN LITTLE LONGSTONE...

...I DIVULGED MY CUNNING PLAN TO PLACATE MARY WITH A ROMANTIC MEAL AFTER THE SHOW.

WELLDODGE SAT NAV

..UNTIL KEN PRODUCED A SATNAV
HE'D BOUGHT FROM – GUESS WHO?

...BY PAINTING OUR LOUNGE CEILING!

TO KEEP UP OUR SPIRITS, I PERFORMED A NEW SONG ON THE BONNET OF MY AUSTIN AMBASSADOR Y REG...

18. Why Dishwashers Are Rubbish

As readers of my previous book, *Two Margarines and Other Domestic Dilemmas*, may recall, I'm not the biggest fan of the dishwasher. The constant worry of bashing your ankles on the dishwasher door (or even tripping over and bashing yer noddle) while loading or unloading is enough to persuade me that the appliance should be banned from all respectable homes. I'm sorry, but I believe the dishwasher is a flawed invention and, when you've heard the following 'strange but true' tale, I don't see how you'll be able to disagree with me.

Please note: it's a fairly long story, but, despite me being a very busy man, I'm happy to share it with you in full!

My story begins when I was in the kitchen one day, sat upon a bar stool waiting for the toaster to warm up a blueberry pancake. That will have surprised some of you, I imagine – that the Shuttleworth household would consume such exotic dainties as blueberry pancakes. I must admit I raised an eyebrow when Mary bought them from the supermarket. But we do like to push the boat out and experiment sometimes, so nobody should be too shocked by this, and I hope you're not. Besides, I think they were on offer at Morrisons. "But hang on!" I hear you remonstrate. "What the heck has that got to do with dishwashers being rubbish?" Please, my friend, be patient!

To continue… I'd already got the margarine out of the fridge (only one tub in there, thankfully!) and the plate and the knife were lined up on the worktop ready to be used, so there was nothing for me to do but wait for the toaster to pop up once it had warmed through my blueberry pancake. Inevitably, there were a few seconds of nothing going on – of silence and contemplation. Well, so you would think. But it wasn't silent! From somewhere I could hear a rhythmic knocking noise. It was the strangest of sounds. What on earth could it be?

It seemed to be a distant sound, and it gradually dawned on me that it must be a massive anvil in action – the type used to beat flat large sections of metal, pewter or stainless steel in a giant factory. A sound – until only a few decades ago – often to be heard in certain parts of Sheffield, South Yorkshire (where I live, in case you'd forgotten!). I racked my brains to think which 'closed-down steel factory' could have started up production again so suddenly with zero publicity. And as I pondered that, the industrial banging noise seemed to get louder. I suddenly became angry. Well, not angry exactly (the last time that happened was over the torn Weetabix packet in 2011, as you know), but I was pretty miffed. How dare they start up with a noisy anvil on a Sunday of all days! (Yes, it was a Sunday – I omitted to mention that.) The cheeky blighters!

I went outside into the garden, expecting the anvil sound to get louder. But instead it went quieter and then suddenly stopped. Thank goodness, and how amazing! Was it really possible that the factory owner could have heard me moaning about it and suddenly rushed onto the factory floor to tell everyone to stop production? It seems unlikely. More probably, others in the neighbourhood had already complained about the noise, and the factory was now finally bowing to public pressure and halting production.

Whatever the cause, the noise had stopped, and I strolled back inside the house, smiling and revelling in my now peaceful neighbourhood. But guess what? As soon as I got inside, the blinking anvil noise started up again. I couldn't believe it! As I advanced towards the kitchen bin (to deposit a discoloured holly leaf and other 'demetrius' I'd picked up off the kitchen doormat upon re-entering the house) the anvil sound grew ever more deafening. What the heck was happening? I was utterly baffled.

To cut a long story short, it was, erm… it seems really silly to say this but it's absolutely true… it was, erm… oof, I feel embarrassed to admit it… it was the blinking dishwasher making the noise! I suspect one or two of you might have guessed that already, but I didn't at all and I feel extremely foolish for not doing so. You see, Mary had put the dishwasher on a few minutes earlier on a long cycle and that arm thingy that whirs round spraying water onto the dishes was catching slightly on an upturned cake tin, creating a repetitive metallic thud that resembled the sound of an anvil in a factory.

How do I know that? Because – my suspicions aroused – I opened the dishwasher door and saw the revolving arm slow down and come to a standstill, leaving no anvil noise – just the sound of dripping water. Once I closed the dishwasher door again the anvil noise resumed. What an idiot I'd been! Fancy being duped like that!

I opened the dishwasher door again and repositioned the cake tin to eradicate the anvil noise, but it was still there, banging away! A slightly different sound now though – like a smaller anvil or a tamping machine (also known as a ballast tamper and often deployed to make newly laid railway tracks level). Did you know that, readers? And did you know that some modern tamping machines are also known as tamper-liners? Fascinating stuff, I'm sure you'll agree, and my thanks go to my wife Mary for letting me use her tablet to find that out!

Back to my story, if you please! Eventually, I managed to place the cake tin at an angle where the water was barely glancing it and so produced no anvil sound. Phew! But by now the dishwasher cycle had almost ended and, yes, with hindsight I should have removed the cake tin entirely as it was clean enough by now. But hindsight is a wonderful thing, and it's easy to say, "John, you big nana!" I wouldn't blame you if you did. "Well, at least you had your blueberry pancake to look forward to, John!" you may also be saying with an encouraging smile, and if so, thanks for remembering that because I'd forgotten myself, having got so wrapped up in the search for the anvil sound. But once I'd solved the mystery, I chuckled to myself as I suddenly remembered there was a blueberry pancake in the toaster. I pressed down the lever on the toaster to reheat it, before resuming my position on the bar stool to wait for the pancake to heat through. Silence once more...

To be fair, for a few seconds I enjoyed the absence of the 'anvil' noise, as it allowed me to concentrate on listening out for the click of the toaster as it completed its heating cycle. Also, if any strange bangs or shouts were to have occurred (suggesting a crime might be being committed nearby), then I'd be the first to know about it, and the first on the scene, although I did still have my slippers on, so hopefully someone else would have been 'first responder'. But there were no sounds and, do you know what, pretty soon it began to 'do me head in, big time' (as my daughter Karen would say). In a nutshell, I was missing the anvil sound, wasn't I? Hearing it had made me deeply nostalgic for the glory years of Sheffield's industrial past. We have little enough industry in the UK as it is nowadays, and although my blueberry pancake popped up and was ready to be eaten, I totally ignored it and set about trying to re-establish the anvil noise by opening the dishwasher door again and repositioning the cake tin.

But guess what? No matter what angle I put the cake tin at, the anvil noise did not resume. I tried for ages, adjusting the tin slightly, then shutting the dishwasher door and cocking my ear and listening out for that lovely industrial sound, then opening the door and trying again. But no matter what position the cake tin was in, the anvil sound had – it seemed – gone for ever. Ironic, in't it, readers, as the real anvil sounds of British industry have more or less gone too. But it's a poor show if you can't recreate the sound in your own blinking dishwasher, in't it? They occur only when you don't expect them to, and the fact that you can't control the 'anvil noise' only strengthens my belief that DISHWASHERS ARE A LOAD OF RUBBISH! Not only are you *not* guaranteed an 'anvil' noise, but you get absolutely drenched continually opening and shutting the dishwasher door trying to adjust the cake tin.

Eventually, I'd had enough and got off my (sore) hands and (aching) knees. With my trousers wet through I stood up and… tripped over the open dishwasher door! Yep, I kid ye not. In my haste to return to the toaster and extract my blueberry pancake, I'd forgotten to close the dishwasher door. Did I fall forward and stab myself on an upturned knife in the cutlery drawer? No, because I always make sure the handles are pointing upwards and you should do that too, for obvious safety reasons. I nearly landed on the cake tin though, which would have been fitting, as I was sick of it, and would have been quite happy to put a dent in it. Mary would have been furious though, so I'm relieved I didn't.

Note: for more detailed info on how to avoid tripping over the dishwasher door, buy a copy of my previous book, *Two Margarines and Other Domestic Dilemmas*, or one of my tea towels (it has the relevant advice printed on it!).

Go on, have a laugh at my misfortune. I won't hold it

against you. But have some sympathy for my poor ankles, and for the loss of the anvil sound and big industry of the past which gave employment to lots of people, and even young kiddies too! Yep, apparently they used to be allowed to work in the factories back in the day. I feel sorry for today's youngsters – banned from working in factories and with no knowledge of how to spin a top or manipulate a hoop with a stick. (Mind you, neither do I. I'm not that old, you know!) Instead, today's youngsters have to stay indoors and play computer games. They don't even have multipacks of Club Biscuits because they've been discontinued, along with the Aztec Bar and more recently the Breakaway (see the next chapter for more info on discontinued sweeties!).

But they do have blueberry pancakes, which is more than I had that day. You see – having been reheated for the seventh time – it came out of the toaster all shrivelled up, overly crispy and most unappetising, and there were no more left in the packet.

Let's finish this chapter with a song that invokes happy memories of the quiet uneventful daytimes of yesteryear, before dishwashers blighted our lives and the 'second post' was a major event, allowing you never to feel…

Alone With the Day

I open the shed door
And forget what I came for
It can't be a deckchair
It's cloudy today
Was it the Brasso
Or the case for my Casio?
It can't have been very important, you say

The Malaysian student
Next door is a true gent
He bids me good morning
As he pegs out his jeans
I would like to speak more
But I have to leave, for
My coffee awaits me, plus two gypsy creams

(Just two, 'cause three would be greedy...)

I love the spirit of daytime
Oh, but sometimes I must say
It gets a little bit boring
Alone with the day

A trip to the lavatory
Lessens my gravity
For I can hear voices when I pull the chain

The cistern refilling
Is relatives milling
And suddenly I'm happy again

I spray the 'tomaters'
Catch the end of *The Archers*
I open some gloss paint
And find it's gone hard
The letterbox goes 'thud'
The lunchtime post's come – good!
But what's that on the mat? Drat! A minicab card!

(In fact, it's three… Don't they know this is a private residence?)

I love the spirit of daytime
Oh, but sometimes I must say
I get a little bit maudlin
Alone with the day

19. Butterscotch Hotch Potch

I mentioned Aztec Bars and Breakaway Bars in the last chapter, and how dreadfully we miss them in our daily lives. But what about butterscotch? It's not been banned or discontinued – as far as I'm aware – but where has all the butterscotch gone? At one time everybody was walking around sucking on a butterscotch. You can laugh, but they were. "Have you crunched into yours yet?" That's what you'd say to a schoolfriend, and it was the Keiller Butterscotch which reigned supreme for many years during the 1960s and early seventies. It boasted a posh wrapper of a light gold colour which shimmered like burnished brass. The inside of the wrapper had a white paper backing which looked reassuringly hygienic. I used to love unwrapping those butterscotch sweeties and popping them into my mouth. And sucking them too, obviously. But never crunching on them. Oof, no, they were far too luxurious for that!

In recent decades butterscotch seems to have disappeared from sweetshop shelves, just like so many other fabulous sweets and chocolate bars, and often we don't know why.

It can lead to a lot of bafflement and sadness and ultimately poor mental health, so before I continue my homage to butterscotch, let's reflect for a moment on some of those other lost gems. Remember the Bar Six? I loved it, but Ken Worthington claims it was discontinued because it was considered too boring. Can that really be true? I thought it was fascinating – an oblong bar of biscuit covered in chocolate and separable into six pieces, hence its highly descriptive name, 'Bar Six'.

Spangles – hmm, I don't know why they disappeared. They were fantastic – especially the cola ones. Does *anybody* know why the Spangle disappeared? When I mentioned it to Ken he looked genuinely shocked that they were no more, turning ashen and repeatedly saying, "They're still around, aren't they? Surely they're still around!" No, Ken, they're not, as I've already stated!!

Remember the Cabana? That's gone an'all. A heady mix of caramel, coconut and cherry cacao wreathed in milk chocolate. I never bought one – far too posh and pricey. I also found the name Cabana slightly intimidating. No, if I wanted an exotic experience I saved up for a Bounty bar – with cardboard tray (more of that shortly!). And what about Fry's Turkish Delight? As a schoolboy I remember regarding them warily on the newsagent's shelf, sensing they were just too sophisticated for a young lad like me. Also – hailing from the Orient as they did – I worried they may contain illegal spices and tinctures that might upset my digestive system. It's the same with Old Jamaica chocolate. I remember eating a piece of it once and worrying that it might get me drunk (the raisins were allegedly laced with rum!) and so make me topple off my friend Lawrence's pogo stick!

When Ski yoghurts first appeared, everyone got excited because they seemed so exotic, and when I first had one I honestly thought it wouldn't be long before I'd be going skiing. That's the power of advertising for you! But it didn't happen. Looking back, I reckon I buried a lot of anger about that. But it all disappeared when hazelnut yoghurts arrived, because everyone went, "Oo, I didn't know you could do that with a yoghurt – put hazelnuts in it!" But you can, and they did, and for a while they were all the rage, and Ski yoghurts suffered in popularity. Good – it serves the company right for deluding young children and making them think they'd all be going on skiing holidays. They should have been banned, but they're still around, as far as I'm aware.

The Topic has gone too, but at least the manufacturers, Mars, prepared us for this event by gradually making it smaller. Do you remember? For years it had been "A hazelnut in every bite" and it suddenly became around 0.7 of a hazelnut. It's a mean trick that sweet manufacturers are employing increasingly. When they did it to the Toblerone I was confused, because although there was a public outcry, I considered a bigger gap between segments to be a massive improvement. In the past my fingers would get trapped in the narrow gap between the chocolate segments of the Toblerone as I tried to break them apart so I could (reluctantly) hand one over to a friend or relative. Unless your fingers could be freed quickly, the warmth from them would start to melt the chocolate, and then you'd have a right mess on your hands

– literally! Widening the gap between segments solved this problem, so initially I didn't understand why people didn't like the revamped 'wide gap' Toblerone. I get it now, and share the public's concern that we're getting less chocolate for our money. Having said that, I'm secretly grateful to Mondelez International for widening the gap between Toblerone segments and keeping my fingers clean!

Just to change the topic back to a different topic – the topic of the Topic again. (Oof, sorry, that doesn't read very well, but it can't be helped.) Ken Worthington has a sinister explanation as to why the Topic was made smaller. Would you like to hear it? Very well. Ken believes that by continually reducing the size of the Topic bar, Mars were hoping it would eventually become undetectable to the naked eye so consumers simply wouldn't notice when it was scrapped. Just think about that for a moment. If it's true, then it's utterly disgraceful that Mars could actually think consumers could be so stupid as to not notice that something has almost become invisible. What do you think? It does seem incredible, I know, but it also makes perfect sense. After all, 45 years ago (is it really so long?) they got rid of the cardboard tray in the Bounty and assumed nobody would notice, or care. Well, I did, and I wrote a protest song about it, which, although it hasn't led to the reinstatement of the cardboard tray, always goes down well at the drop-in centre, where much 'air punching' accompanies the chorus. Feel free to do the same, readers!

Mutiny Over the Bounty

In the past
Bounty bars were head and shoulders above the
rest
'Cause they were built to last
The cardboard strip
Wasn't just for show, oh no, the Bounty fit
Like a glove in it

Giving the fragile coconut bars
Much-needed protection
I can't believe those men from Mars
Would vote for its rejection

Oh, Mars of Slough,
You've really done it now
You've seen fit to remove the strip
Of cardboard from the Bounty
Oh, Mars of Slough,
I'm sorry but from now
I'm a Cadbury's man, a Bounty fan
You can no longer count me

You might think
Once the Bounty bar was eaten that would be it
For the cardboard strip

But no, once pressed
It made a very attractive bookmark or failing this...
A sturdy shopping list

What fool said, "Lets scrap the card"?
I don't understand it
You would think those men from Mars
Were from another planet!

And so to close, what I propose
Without being unduly rowdy
Is a mutiny over the Bounty!

(Let's boycott all Mars products until they reinstate the cardboard strip! Oof! It won't be easy, 'cause they're quite tasty, aren't they?)

Oh, Mars of Slough,
You've really done it now
You've seen fit to remove the strip
Of cardboard from the Bounty
Oh, Mars of Slough,
I'm sorry but from now
I'm a Rowntree's man, a Bounty fan
You can no longer count me

MUTINY OVER THE BOUNTY!!!

I've just remembered, in the seventies there was briefly a butterscotch pastille issued by Rowntree's, but I fear it wasn't around for long. Oof, I keep going on about butterscotch, but I realise anyone under the age of 45 might not be familiar with that flavour. Except… what am I saying? The butterscotch flavour lives on, of course it does… in Angel Delight! Yes, my favourite flavour is the butterscotch one (apart from the strawberry flavour, and the banana one possibly…)

In the absence of butterscotch sweeties, what can one safely suck on in contemporary society? Well, these days I make do with the Werther's Original, and it's no hardship – they're an excellent substitute for butterscotch although not quite as posh, and this is reflected in a sensible retail price that makes that sweetie accessible to all. However, I don't enjoy eating them in the presence of my wife, Mary, because she always asks for one when I've hardly got any left (but I feel obliged to let her have one anyway!). Then, within a few seconds she's crunching into it almost violently. Honestly, it breaks my heart to hear how rapidly the sweet is demolished by Mary's jaws. You may say I'm overreacting, and you may be right, but I can't help my feelings, and I shouldn't disguise my upset, should I? It's not healthy to bury strong emotions – Joan Chitty keeps telling me that. Sorry to go on. It's just that I fervently believe Werther's – and indeed any hard-boiled sweet (including both the Murray and Everton mint) – should be sucked slowly and mindfully. There, I've said it, and I feel I can let the chapter end now.

20. What a Spectacle!

My favourite moment at the opticians is always after I've chosen my frames and I'm guided to a little cubicle with a desk by an optician's assistant, and then swiftly abandoned. "That sounds awful" I hear you cry. "Why would you choose that as your favourite moment at the opticians – just after you've been abandoned?" But the point is, the abandonment is never for long. I know that pretty soon someone will attend to me. "Someone will be with you shortly, duckie," the lady always says before she abandons me. You see? So I sit and wait for another lady to come with the clipboard and try the frames on so she can make subtle adjustments.

"What were you doing at the opticians, John? I thought you had 20/20 vision," I hear some of you cry. Ah, I think I know to what you're referring – it's the song I sang at the start of my 2020 tour – *John Shuttleworth's Back*. But that's why I said I had '2020 vision'. I was trying to be witty. Apologies if I misled you – my eyesight's actually terrible. However, as I've already mentioned it, let's refresh our memories and sing a little of that quirky ditty:

Old Four Eyes Is Back

Old Four Eyes is back
With 20/20 vision
I haven't lost the knack
Of playing the fun rhythm
But John Shuttleworth's back
Oo, the gyp that it has given
I pray though
It's just lumbago
If it's a slipped disc
I shouldn't risk this
But I'm a trouper
And it is true, yeah,
Old Four Eyes is back!

Oof, it was a difficult time, just before lockdown, and – never mind my bad eyesight – it was my back giving me cause for concern then. Years of strenuous DIY and playing the organ while perched upon a multi-pack of Diet Sprite in my garage is what did the damage. No lumbar support, you see. It brought on my sciatica, and then I'd have to go and have a lie down – and imbibe a Diet Sprite, which of course made my seat (now minus a can) more precarious and less supportive, and my back problems worse. Some may argue that I should be furious with Diet Sprite for what happened to my back and put in a claim for millions of pounds, but do you not think I've thought of that already? If I tried to sue them for a huge sum (plus a lifetime supply of Diet Sprite – it would be crazy not to ask for that too!), well, honestly, I'd be laughed out of court.

Where were we? Oh yes, at the opticians, but I'd like to leave there, if I may, because I've become bored with talking about it. I'd rather discuss the problems of trying to reach for your glass of water during the night in the dark. Oof, I'm always knocking over my glass of water in the night. Mary doesn't like me putting on the light, you see, which is fair enough, I suppose, but it does mean when I wake up with a parched throat I have to fish for my water glass by making small exploratory hand movements. Then when I think I'm getting close, I slowly spread open my hand to resemble a claw with my fingers wide apart and move it purposefully towards where I think the glass is. It's a hit-and-miss affair and not unlike those machines in motorway service stations where you try to win a soft toy.

You'd think, therefore, it would be fun trying to find my water glass and I might be chuckling to myself as I did it? Well, no, you're very wide of the mark there. Firstly, if I ever chuckled, Mary would wake up instantly and demand to know what I was chuckling at. (It happened once when I couldn't sleep but had just recalled a quip made by Duncan 'Chase Me' Norville on *Blankety Blank*.) Secondly, those arcade games with the claw are *not* fun, so I wouldn't be chuckling anyway. If you've ever tried it yourself, you'll know it's a miserable experience which always ends in failure. So does reaching for my water glass. The only good thing, I suppose, is I don't have to spend a pound every time I reach for my glass. Imagine if you did – it would be intolerable!

Even if I did have perfect vision, I'd struggle to locate my glass in the night because I'm in a very groggy state with having only just woken up, so my coordination is poor. Locating my Rennies in the night in the event of heartburn is similarly difficult, but I make things easy for myself… By doing what exactly? Shall I tell you? I think indigestion sufferers will be very grateful to hear my little tip and will want to adopt it. The tip is this: if you know you'll need a Rennie in the night, or any type of indigestion relief tablet that comes in a blister pack, pierce the foil of the pack and extract the tablet before you go to sleep. The reason you must do this is that in the dead of night piercing a foil blister pack can make a heck of a racket and will wake up your partner as easily as if you start chuckling. Coughing's alright

– you can't help that. But no chuckling, or sighing for that matter, or making clucking noises with your tongue. And no piercing of foil, please. Line up your Rennies at bedtime and do sleep well… and please don't have nightmares.

Oof, we seem to be onto night-time tips, so here's another. If you have to answer the call of nature during the night, move as silently and stealthily as possible to avoid waking anyone sleeping next to you or even just in the same room. Avoid clambering back into the bed too boisterously as your momentum might cause you to bash your elbow into your sleeping wife's head. I did that once and woke poor Mary up. So now I try to creep softly and slither into bed. A bit like a snake? Yes, though obviously there's no need to hiss as you settle back under the covers.

As we've mentioned snakes – I can't remember which James Bond film it is where a poisonous snake comes into James's bedroom late at night. It slithers in (just like me getting back into bed), and luckily the quick-thinking Mr Bond sees it in the mirror and sets light to a can of hair spray with which he burns the snake to death. I'd obviously not be happy if Mary did that to me, but there's always a small chance she could, as she has an extensive range of hair products and there's a lighter in our bedroom for when Mary lights her aromatherapy candle that Joan Chitty bought her for Christmas in 2021.

Back to 'spectacle' matters – I just want to say that one of the most frustrating things about the modern kagoule is that the hood always seems too big and inevitably it flops over your face, obscuring your vision, even if you've got your specs on, and causes you to bump into other shoppers hurrying to escape a sudden rain shower. Or it could be hikers you collide with if you're out on Kinder Scout or even just in the car park of the Pencil Museum in Keswick as you hurry to the cafe to avoid a downpour. The ideal solution is to gather up the excess material at the back of the hood and trap it with a clothes peg. This has the double advantage of restoring normal vision by raising the hood line to above your eyes and providing a peg with which you can later secure the kagoule to the washing line in order to dry it.

A note of caution: once I got the Velcro of my kagoule cuff caught in Mary's hair. She wasn't happy, as it took several minutes to disentangle her. It would have been quicker but obviously I only had one hand available to conduct the detangling process. The other hand was dangling helplessly next to Mary's head like it was attached to a withered arm. Oof… it was awful, and a miserable few minutes were spent until Mary was finally free. Luckily, my wife sports a short low-maintenance bob in the shape of a motorcycle helmet. If she'd had a large frizzy mane like that jazz singer lady, Cleo Laine, had, or even a bubble perm like Ken Worthington, the situation might have been even graver.

Right, I'd like to end with a brand-new song all about a common dilemma: what do you do if you need to find your spectacles but you can't start looking for them until you can see properly and in order to do that you need to find your blinking specs. Oo, it's a tough one!

Spectacle Song

I need to find my spectacles
So I can find my spectacles
I've been scouring shelves and rifling drawers
Up on tiptoe, down on all fours
But I cannot detect at all
My spectacles. So heed this call
The saddest of all spectacles
Is a man searching for spectacles!

Until I find my spectacles
So I can look for my spectacles
My life's on hold, and I admit
I almost feel like ending it
I really do not need this
I need my ruddy readers!
(Oof, beg your pardon, I mean…
I need my READY readers!)
To put it more politely
Please reunite me
With my blinking specs!!

The saddest of all spectacles
Is a man searching for spectacles
I've been scouring shelves and rifling drawers
Up on tiptoe, down on all fours
But I can't find my spectacles

So how WILL I find my spectacles?
And I NEED to find my spectacles
So I can watch *An Inspector Calls*

(That's an old film that was on the telly that night. Ken Worthington had recommended it – supposed to be a classic, but once I eventually found my specs, I watched it for five minutes and realised it was extremely boring. Slow-moving, old-fashioned and in black and white an' all – what a rip-off! So I turned over to watch *Gladiators* hosted by crack father-and-son presenter team Bradley and Barney Walsh. An exquisite pairing, if ever I saw one. Incidentally, despite what I said earlier, the door is still open for Bradley to visit and claim that complimentary meal for one. Just give us a couple of hours' notice, Brad, so we can Hoover, prepare veg, etc.)

RBM and Chic Ken Productions present the motion picture...

IT'S NICE UP NORTH

with John Shuttleworth

filmed by MARTIN PARR

21.
The Man Who Ate His Wife's Tea

There's a friend of my wife Mary called Patricia Macmahon, who works on an open-air market selling sundry items such as gaffer tape, balls of string, that sort of thing. Cigarette papers, erm… candles? No, she doesn't do candles, actually, but she should do. Erm… lighters, yes, she does them, five for a pound.

Anyhow, in wintertime Patricia sports a lovely padded coat with a big hood edged with fur (like what that little lad off *South Park* used to wear). That's not on the telly any more, that programme. Good, because it wasn't my cup of tea, but do you remember the type of hood I mean? Very curled round the face so the head resides well back in the hood (as if at the end of a tunnel). I truly admire the design of the hood, but there's one problem I have with it. If ever I want to talk directly to Patricia and establish eye contact – in order to negotiate the price of a reel of duct tape, for instance – it's incredibly difficult. You have to face Patricia square on and peer down her hood to try and see her face at the far end. But you can't because it's immersed in darkness. Ideally, you'd point a torch down there, but she might be blinded and become hostile. But my point is – you can't read her expression to tell if the price you've offered is acceptable. Although, to be fair, she always says to me in a weary voice, "The prices of my wares are all clearly marked, John, as you well know." And then she'll turn away to serve somebody else, so I guess that's me told!

Sorry to go on about the hood, as it has absolutely nothing to do with the story, but it seemed an interesting way to introduce Patricia, who is a chief protagonist in this sorry tale. She used to be married to Barry Macmahon (the other chief protagonist), a painter and decorator by trade. About 25 years ago, Barry became very slow in his work, and as a result stopped being offered jobs, which eventually led to clinical depression. He was taking a week to paint a small garden gate, which I'm sure you'll agree is totally unacceptable.

So depressed became Barry that one evening he did the unthinkable – he ate his wife Patricia's tea while she was in the hall on the phone to her mother. Mary told me this after meeting Patricia outside the arcade the following day, and apparently she was still shaking with anger. For Mary to know that, Patricia can't have been wearing the coat with the hood. Or at least she must've had the hood down so Mary could monitor her expression and observe her shaking. (Having said that, if her shaking was violent, it would surely have been transferred through the whole coat, including the hood, and be detectable to Mary, so perhaps the hood was up?)

Anyhow, Patricia told Mary that she was out of the kitchen

for just a few minutes, and when she came back she found her tea (fish fingers, chips and beans) had been gobbled up by Barry. He finished his own tea first, obviously. That would have been a bit weird – to start on someone else's meal before finishing your own. Interesting, though, isn't it – how 'Slow Barry' suddenly managed to speed up when food became involved? If he ate at the speed he painted, he'd only have had time to steal a few chips and maybe half a fish finger, and Patricia wouldn't have been that bothered. (Alternatively, if Barry painted at the speed he ate – well, he'd have a full order book, I'm sure!)

But what a crazy thing to do – to eat your wife's tea… without her permission, anyway. I occasionally have one of Mary's new potatoes, or even a sprout, but only at the invitation of Mary, and with her full and continued assurance that she doesn't mind. "Are you sure you don't mind, love?" I'll ask. And I do that three times. Firstly, as I stab the potato or sprout with my fork and transfer it from Mary's to my plate; secondly, just before I eat it – you know, as my food-laden fork is hovering just outside my mouth; and then thirdly and finally, when the potato or sprout (or half a hash brown it was once!) is actually in my mouth and on its way down to my tummy. Because my mouth's full, Mary can't always hear what I've said, so I often have to repeat it a couple of times which can make her annoyed. In future, I might not bother with asking her the third time; as well as riling Mary unnecessarily, it's clearly too late to give the food back to her. And there's one more reason I shouldn't be asking Mary at that point. Have you spotted the reason, readers? Come on… think hard (but hopefully not too hard, as it's blinking obvious!). No? You can't guess? Okay, I'll tell yer… it's very rude to talk with your mouth full, that's why!

Back to the fascinating story of The Man Who Ate His Wife's Tea. When she spied her empty plate, Patricia was furious with her errant husband, and justifiably so. Barry said, "I'm so sorry, love. I don't know why I did that. But let me go and buy you a takeaway." So off Barry went to the local Chinese to get Patricia a takeaway. However, when he returned with the takeaway she didn't want to eat it because she was still so angry with him. So erm… Barry ate that as well! So then what do you think he did? He went for a lie down on the sofa (totally understandable as he must have been severely bloated!). He turned to the wall and lay all evening just looking at the wall, blinking. Oof, how awful…

After his divorce from Patricia (well, how could they ever recover from an incident like that?), Barry moved into his own flat and made bird tables for a while (I trust he painted them as well? Oof, no, that would have taken too long, so I hope he didn't!). But although Barry has now retired, he still paints. But not like he used to. "Oo, do you mean he's speeded up?" you're wondering. No, on the contrary – he probably paints slower than ever!

Confused? Let me explain. Barry no longer paints banisters, gates or window frames, etc. He now paints animals on your wall. *"Animals on your wall?"* I hear you cry. Yes, like a mural. He copies them from a photo, and only if you ask him to and give him £150 (or £225 for two walls). But they're very good, apparently. Oof, who would have thought that a painter and decorator would have any artistic leanings? But Barry clearly has, and I'm happy for him. I last saw him in the arcade wearing a bushwhacker hat which made him look very stylish, although as he took long hard puffs on his vaper and stared into the distance you could sense he was still a bit down. The fact that Patricia doesn't talk to him any more doesn't help, I suppose, but can you blame her? He stole her tea!

Barry's latest commission is – wait for it – a sabre-toothed tiger! He's not started it yet, and, frankly, I hope he doesn't. You see, it's to be painted on Joan Chitty's bathroom wall, and we're concerned that she's making a terrible mistake agreeing to it. Mary said she should go for a budgie (to remind her of Les) or an otter or something nice and reassuring, but Joan seems hellbent on having a sabre-toothed tiger in her blinking bathroom – a giant one an' all covering the whole of the wall. Is she mad? Mary and I both think possibly so. The thing is, although Joan's currently displaying no mental health issues, what will she be like after a few night-time encounters with the sabre-toothed tiger? Honestly, Joan has made some foolish decisions in her time, but this latest one surely takes the biscuit!

We've already had that song (about taking the biscuit), so let's conclude this fascinating chapter with a song celebrating Joan's 'best ever' decision: buying a Citroën Berlingo. Good on you, Joan. I'm madly jealous, and I can't pretend I'm not…

Berlingo

I covet Joan's Berlingo
Heated seats and big window
Boy, look at that thing go
I covet Joan's Berlingo

I covet Joan's Berlingo
Boy, look at that thing go
Feels like I've won at bingo
When I'm driving her Berlingo

What of my Austin Ambassador?
I've spent so much of my past with her
It would hurt and embarrass her
If she knew I was thinking of scrapping her

I covet Joan's Berlingo
Heated seats and big window
Boy, look at that thing go
I covet Joan's Berlingo

What of my Werther's Originals?
Well, the Berlingo has lots of pigeonholes
Think of the Werther's Originals
I could store in those pigeonholes!

I covet Joan's Berlingo

More than any car? Yes, I think so
Boy, look at that thing go
I covet Joan's Berlingo
Yes, I covet Joan's Berlingo!

(Ultimately, I believe I'm still best off with my Austin Ambassador. I may not have all those pigeonholes, but I do have a magical glove compartment which, when it's opened, allows your bag of travel sweets to slide down effortlessly onto the – now horizontal – open door ready for immediate access. I doubt whether the Berlingo or indeed any other vehicle on this Earth has that amazing facility. Bless you, little Y Reg!)

22. Shock Around the Clock

A few months ago, US singer Bill Haley was on an old edition of *Top of the Pops* singing a song you might just have heard of: 'Rock Around The Clock'. I have to be honest and admit that for years I never enjoyed that song, and hearing it always made me anxious. "How so, John?" many – if not all – readers will be wondering. Fair enough, I can't blame you wanting to know how that classic tune could make me anxious, which it did, as I've already stated. Hmm, it's slightly embarrassing, this, but I've started the story so I guess I'm going to have to continue with it. The song made me anxious because I always assumed Bill Haley was singing about dancing around an actual clock. Let's face it – that's what he says they're going to do. "We're going to rock around the clock tonight." And so I thought if they did that, there was a very real danger that the clock would get trodden on or damaged in some way. And that's what made me anxious. There's always one idiot, isn't there – not looking where they're stepping? In addition, and this made me anxious too, the thought that someone was going to have to take a clock down from a shelf or even unscrew it from a wall (and, I trust, store the screws in a safe place for the duration of the dancing) and then be positioning the clock in the centre of a dance floor – just to have a blinking dance! What a kerfuffle! Why do it? It seemed crazy, and still does.

During the recent TV screening of the song I confided in my wife Mary my misgivings about the song and its message, and stressed yet again how impractical Bill Haley's idea to dance around a clock actually was. Initially, Mary looked at me like I was mad, and then she slowly explained that Bill wasn't singing about dancing around an actual clock. Instead, he meant that they would be dancing for a long time. I suddenly realised that made perfect sense, and my earlier conclusion may have been awry. But can I just say, in my defence, when I first heard the song I was only a young lad and I'd never heard the expression 'around the clock' and so I naturally assumed he meant dancing around the clock itself. I get it now, and am indebted to Mary for explaining things and putting me right. In addition, once she realised I wasn't winding her up (oof, sorry, I didn't mean to say that pun – very funny!) I got to see Mary laugh like I've not seen her laugh since we were in a rowing boat in the early eighties (while we were courting) and I lost an oar. She threw her head back and laughed herself silly, which was lovely to see, even though I also saw quite a few of her fillings (which she didn't have the time we were in the boat, or she might just have had one back then).

Now the dust has settled and I've had time to reflect on the incident – although I feel slightly foolish, and I accept that Mary's explanation makes perfect sense – part of me suspects that Bill Haley might be having a laugh at our expense. He's *probably* singing about dancing all day and night, I accept that. But he just *might be* singing about dancing around an actual clock for a very long period! And what's more – he *might* even be planning to damage the face of the clock with his winklepickers! I know Bill's not around now to defend himself, so it's a bit unfair, I suppose, to accuse him of that, but it's just possible he was up to no good. Anything else that convinces me of this? Yes, there is… Bill Haley was always laughing when he sang the song, wasn't he? Or at least grinning excessively. Why? Dancing all day and night isn't something that would put a smile on anyone's face, is it? A frown maybe, or a yawn! He was having a laugh, stringing everyone along and ultimately taking us all for fools. Thank goodness one or two of us have managed to see right through him!

I think we'll leave it there, shall we? But hopefully from now on you'll keep more of an open mind about the true meaning of certain classic rock song lyrics. Let's end with another rock song – this one's all about a pumice stone (well, that's a rock, in't it?) which used to be next to the bath for years until one day it mysteriously disappeared. I suspect my wife Mary may have had a hand in this, but upon being quizzed she denied all knowledge of the stone's disappearance. I think she's not telling the entire truth (as Bill Haley didn't about his flagship composition), but I've no proof, so I've deemed it judicious to keep my suspicions private, and I'd appreciate it if you'd do the same. However, feel free to sing along with this song.

Ken says the song has an anthemic quality which has encouraged me to send a cassette copy to that lad from Coldplay with the curly hair who seems extremely approachable. Chris something, is it? He has a slightly dopey grin but looks like he'd agree to anything, so I've a good feeling about a potential collaboration. I'm led to believe that Chris (or is it Martin?) has a spiritual curiosity which this song will satisfy, mentioning – as it does – the moon. Hope to hear from you soon, Chris! Don't be like Bradley Walsh and blank me – please get back pronto and we can start the ball rolling! My next-door neighbour and sole agent Ken Worthington is eagerly awaiting your call!

The Pumice Stone

I'm proud to say I once did own,
I once did own a pumice stone
It had no rope attached as some
Pumice stones do. Not this one.

I never felt I was alone
At bathtime with my pumice stone
I loved it so, it worked a treat
In removing hard skin from my feet

Many a night I'd sit and gaze
Upon my pumice stone as I bathed
So strange a rock I was inclined
To think that from the moon it had been mined

But constant use wore it away
It became a smaller stone each day
And so was easier to lose
Among all my wife's various shampoos

One night my pumice stone I sought
To pare a callous on my foot
But it had gone and in its place a
Gadget that resembled a cheese grater

I'm proud to say I once did own,
I once did own a pumice stone
Although it's gone I hope that soon
It will land safely back on the moon

23. We Saw the New Year in in an Inn

CHRISTMAS WAS DULL, MY TUMMY GOT TOO FULL
BUT WE SAW THE NEW YEAR IN IN AN INN.

UT WE SAW THE NEW
AR IN IN AN INN.

CHRISTMAS, WE HATED, AND AS I'VE ALREADY STATED
WE SAW THE NEW YEAR IN IN AN INN.

CAROLS

THE INN WAS VERY FLASHY,
THE CARVERY WAS CLASSY,
THE MEAT WAS CARVED BY A LADY,
THEN WE HELPED OURSELVES TO GRAVY.

AND WHEN SHE SAW THE SWEET TROLLEY
MY WIFE SAID 'GOODNESS GOLLY!'

AND IT'S FAIR TO INFER THAT THE FAYRE WAS FAR FROM JUST FAIR... YOU KNOW – IT WAS FANTASTIC!
HRISTMAS WAS GRIM, UT WE'RE ABLE TO GRIN, OR WE SAW THE NEW EAR IN IN AN INN.
'S DIFFICULT TO SAY, BUT I'LL SAY IT ANYWAY – 'E SAW THE NEW YEAR IN IN AN INN.

24. The Annoying Baby

Ken Worthington recently told me something that some folk may find amusing. I suppose it is, vaguely, but upsetting and frustrating too if you were there witnessing the strange goings on that afternoon in the hotel banqueting hall. It was Janet Le Roe's parents' Golden Wedding Anniversary and a sumptuous spread had been provided for the 100-plus guests at the luxurious hotel in the South Yorkshire village which must remain nameless (only because I've forgotten the name). Now, which village did Ken say it was? Was it Tickhill? No. Was it Thurcroft? I don't think so. Thurgoland? Don't be silly. Oof, was it Clowne? Gringley on the Hill? Don't be daft… that's getting towards Gainsborough on the A631. Look, I'm sorry, I can't remember where the celebration was held. What I *do* know is that I wasn't invited. Why not? Janet is a stablemate and we could have performed a few songs together – me on my organ and Janet on her acoustic guitar (Janet can do finger picking, remember, readers – an awesome skill of which I'm hugely admiring).

Then, after the performance, I could have sat down (perhaps at a separate table away from the main guests) and been given a plateful of savoury dainties and a soft drink (and a napkin, obviously!). I'd have been quite happy with that – *plus* my petrol money. That's the least I would expect in lieu of a performance fee. However, for reasons best known to herself, Janet chose not to invite me. That's fine, I don't really know Janet anyway and I certain don't know her parents. But let's put any potential animosity firmly to one side and say, "Congratulations to Terry and Lorna Roebottom for achieving half a century of marriage!"

The eagle-eyed will have noticed that while Janet is called Le Roe, her parents have a 'bottom' and no 'Le'. This is because Janet was encouraged by her agent (and mine!), a Mr Ken Worthington of WINTA (Worthington's International New Talent Agency), to drop 'bottom' and put 'Le' at the front. Ken's ingenious plan was to increase Janet's international appeal on the Northern Carvery circuit. And, boy, has it reaped dividends! Janet was checked out for a carpet-shop promotion on the Isle of Wight just before the pandemic. She famously played Alan-a-Dale in an all-female production of *Robin Hood* at Keighley a good few years ago, and, of course, Janet provides musical accompaniment for a storyteller at a Toby Inn in Millhouses. (See Chapter 9, A Tatty Story, for more details!)

But please can we get back to the Golden Wedding party? We've established Janet didn't invite me. But more disturbingly, KEN didn't invite me either. Why would he? Well, Ken is my agent and my next-door neighbour and a dear, dear friend. He travelled to the event alone and yet the status of his invite (I've subsequently learnt) was 'plus one', so, you know, he could have invited me! Mind you, I would have regretted going once I'd had to witness the antics of the baby. That's right, you read that correctly. The antics and indeed the appalling, disruptive and annoying behaviour of THE ANNOYING BABY!

According to Ken, the baby was seated at one end of a table between its parents. (I don't know the name of the baby nor indeed the sex of the infant, and I don't really care, so if you don't mind, we'll continue to refer to it as an 'it'. Or just 'the baby'.) People were tucking into a lovely spread and the wine was flowing, plus soft drinks (which I've no doubt it – the baby – was taking full advantage of!), when suddenly there was a loud banging on the table. Anyone who's attended a wedding or a civil ceremony of any kind knows full well that the sound of a banging spoon means it's time to shut up as the speeches are about to begin. Well, everyone did indeed fall silent and look towards Terry and Lorna Roebottom's table, expecting one or both of them to rise and make a speech. But they didn't. They were deeply engrossed in conversation and clearly not about to make a speech. So after a few seconds people looked away from the couple and the hubbub of chatter began once more. Ken was confused and began looking around the room to locate where the banging spoon sound had originated. Before he could locate it, the blinking spoon banging began again, and as you'd expect… the room fell silent once more. Would Terry rise or would it be Lorna first? Neither. They were still chatting (well, Lorna was; by this time Terry was in the middle of eating a slice of quiche so his mouth was otherwise occupied). But neither were about to stand up and address the guests, so, as before, people resumed chatting, but this time a few people were laughing and pointing too.

Ken looked in the direction of the pointing and saw a big baby who had in its hand a big spoon. Yes – the baby was the culprit! Some foolish adult had equipped the baby with a spoon and so it was banging it at will and wreaking havoc in the banqueting hall. Seconds later the banging began again, but only for a moment this time, as the mum took the spoon off the baby and gave it a breadstick instead. Ken was relieved, but I'm not so sure about the mother's actions at this point. In my day they gave babies a Farley's Rusk to chew on if they needed distracting, but nowadays they give them a bread stick which is surely dangerous. Firstly, isn't there a real risk they could poke someone's eye out with the bread stick? And, even worse, what if the breadstick has broken off at an angle or been bitten off to leave a serrated edge? It seems absolutely crazy to me that the breadstick has been authorised as a safe food product for babies, don't you agree, readers? It also seems crazy to me that the baby had been given a spoon in the first place. Well, at least that problem had been sorted – temporarily!

After a few seconds during which the baby threw the breadstick to the ground (a health and safety-conscious baby, perhaps?) and began wailing, the spoon was placed back in its hand. Such action beggars belief! Ken knew exactly what would happen next – the annoying baby started banging on the table with it again, and this time… guess what? Not a single guest fell silent in anticipation of Lorna and Terry's speech. They just carried on chatting, drinking and eating. And can you blame them? They'd got wise to it, and they'd had enough of being duped by an annoying baby.

Can I just say at this point in defence of the annoying baby – remember it *was* just a baby and probably unaware of the convention of banging a spoon on a table to quieten an audience, so let's not be too hard on it. After all, it was just practising its hand-to-eye coordination and enjoying the loud sound an enticingly glittery metal object could produce when hit against a resonant surface. But at the same time, we shouldn't ignore the fact that its actions were *very* annoying, and wreaking havoc in the banqueting hall, and so *must* be roundly condemned.

The intermittent spoon banging continued unabated for the next few minutes, with none of the guests paying any attention. Meanwhile, Ken Worthington watched anxiously as Terry Roebottom wiped his mouth with his napkin and got ready to stand up and begin his 'speech of thanks'. He waited for a few moments for the crowd to stop chatting, but they didn't, so Terry grabbed a spoon and banged it on the table. No response. He banged it again and still the guests chattered on. At this point, if the baby had been banging its spoon as well, maybe the guests would have heard both spoons being banged and the extra 'banging spoon' volume would have shut them up. But, unfortunately, the baby – startled by hearing a rival spoon being banged – had stopped banging and was just listening to the sound, with one ear cocked (according to Ken).

Terry was struggling. He banged his spoon for ages, but no one paid any attention. Eventually, he yelled out, "Shut up everybody, please, just *shut up*!", which did shut everybody up but – according to Ken – it seemed overly aggressive, and so it definitely soured the atmosphere slightly. As a result, Terry's speech didn't go down very well at all. And guess what? Midway through the speech he was drowned out by another sound – that of a baby crying. Well, if you were a baby and you'd had your spoon taken off you and you were being forced to listen to a boring speech, you'd probably cry, wouldn't you? My sympathies go out to poor Terry Roebottom, but having said that – why oh why did he invite an annoying baby who ruined what might otherwise have been a smashing event?

Hey, I mentioned that the party was in a South Yorkshire hotel, and although I can't remember the village, it wouldn't have been a million miles away from Rotherham. That's a city now, of course, not just a mere town, and a place where I have relatives living. Not that I see them very often. Why not? The best way to explain might be to sing this song with which we will end this slightly harrowing chapter.

Relatives in Rotherham

Relatives in Rotherham
We don't see a lorra them
Tend not to bother them
Those relatives in Rotherham

And when they come to our house
The hours we have to suffer them
The biscuits we have to offer them
Those relatives in Rotherham

Relatives in Rotherham
We don't see a lorra them
Tend not to bother them
Those relatives in Rotherham

When cousin Lyn had a baby
We had to go and visit them
Be hugging and kissing them
Pretend that we'd been missing them

The love you feel for your kids and wife
Keeps you going through this life
But the love you feel for the family that you don't live with
Well, it's relative!

And when they come to our house
The hours we have to suffer them
The biscuits we have to offer them
Those relatives from Rotherham

Relatives in Rotherham
We don't see a lorra them
Tend not to bother them
Those relatives in Rotherham

Oof, relatives in Rotherham!

RBM PRESENTS

John Shuttleworth

in

THE MINOR TOUR

...and other mythological creatures!

Photo: Tony Briggs

"A ludicrously compelling night out"
Evening Standard

PLUS SPECIAL GUESTS

www.shuttleworths.co.uk

25. Shall We Share the Shortbread, Shirley? (The Day I 'Took the Biscuit')

As a boy I used to love children's parties, apart from the party where I ended up eating the wrapper of a fairy cake. I thought it was rice paper, you see, so I began nibbling it, but pretty soon I realised it wasn't edible. It was a wax-based greaseproof paper, and I naturally spat out the partly masticated pieces. Oof, big mistake, spitting out the paper. The host's mother (Mrs, erm… I've no idea, I'm afraid, it was so long ago!) saw me and exclaimed, "Dirty little boy!" and came over and gave me a little smack on my wrist. It sounds abusive, and nowadays would probably be illegal, but back then it was quite common and acceptable. Still, it was a shock and – on top of the disappointment of not being able to eat the cake wrapper – was just too much for me, and I cried my eyes out. After all, I was only five. Anyone else would have done the same at that age. Hmm, or would they? I suspect somebody like Bear Grylls wouldn't have cried at five. He'd have been shocked and bewildered, I'm sure, but would already have developed the technique and self-control to hold back the tears.

But Bear is the exception. I've no doubt that that kind of trauma would have had most lads roaring (and even some little girls!).

After I'd dried my eyes, I got down from the table and went off to play Musical Statues. Remember playing that at children's parties? It was so exciting waiting for the music to stop, and as soon as it did, you had to freeze. Often, you'd think the music *had* stopped (during a quiet passage) and would freeze, only to realise you'd made a grave error and so you'd have to start dancing again. The lovely thing is you never seemed to be penalised for doing that, so I tended to stop quite often, hoping that the law of averages would assist me and eventually one of my 'false freezes' would coincide with the music actually stopping. Wasn't that cheating? Yes, to some extent it was, and I don't condone or excuse my behaviour, but I was a very competitive little lad and always wanted to win – especially Pass the Parcel which I NEVER EVER won!

So, when the music did eventually stop during musical statues, what were your chances of staying in the game? If you were firmly rooted to the ground, perhaps doing a little jive or shoe shuffle, you could stop easily and you knew you wouldn't be out. But if you'd misjudged it – perhaps with one leg up or an arm raised (so your centre of gravity was dangerously high), inevitably you would topple over and you knew you were out; a crushing feeling, and it was hard not to cry (again!). Hmm, would Bear Grylls have cried at the disappointment of being knocked out of Musical Statues? Well, I wouldn't dream of speaking for the popular TV survival expert on this or any other issue, but I reckon he would have blubbered like a baby, and they might even have had to contact his parents at that point so he could be taken home early. Oof, poor Bear – it's hard to imagine him having such a sad early exit, but I'm sure he wouldn't be like that now and would take being knocked out with good grace. Well, I sincerely hope he would now he's a grown man. It would be pitiful if he got stroppy about it and tried to insist he hadn't moved, when clearly he had.

Oranges and Lemons – remember that game? I didn't like it when they sang, "Here comes the chopper to chop off your head!" It was terrifying as various arms used to come down in a scything motion and pretend to chop off your head! To be honest, I used to miss a lot of the games at parties, as I would still be at the tea table having my fill of all the fabulous dainties on display. I could never understand how other children could 'get down' when the plate of potted meat sandwiches wasn't yet empty. Or there were still lots of lovely chocolate tea cakes on the table, or those Party Rings – the perfect platter biscuit, remember them? As for those pink wafer biscuits! Oof, I'm getting hungry again, so maybe I should end by singing a sobering ballad that might quell my hunger while recalling a disturbing childhood party incident. It was an occasion where I did literally 'take the biscuit'.

Shall We Share the Shortbread, Shirley?

I was at a children's party
many years ago
The sandwiches were potted meat
and the lemonade did flow
Most of the children had left the table
to begin the party games
Just me and a lass called Shirley
still eating did remain

I'd finished my jelly and ice cream
and was considering getting down
When I spied a piece of shortbread
As I did so, Shirley frowned
I tried to take the biscuit
but Shirley grabbed the plate
She clearly coveted that cake
so before it was too late (I said)

Shall we share the shortbread, Shirley?
Surely we should!
There's only one piece left
and like to eat it we both would
Shortbread's shaped for sharing
and I'm confident we could
So shall we share the shortbread, Shirley?

Surely we should

Meanwhile a little lad called Len
was getting up to no good
He'd been knocked out of Musical Bumps
and returned to have more grub
He moved in on the shortbread
but that petticoat tail was mine
I gave him a Chinese burn
and how the wimp did whine!

(That wasn't very nice, I know. But I was desperate...)

Shall we share the shortbread, Shirley?
Surely we should!
There's only one piece left
and like to eat it we both would
Shortbread's shaped for sharing
and I'm confident we could
So shall we share the shortbread, Shirley?
Surely we should

Now Carol is Coming inCredibly Close
as William is Warning she Would
Len's still Looming, Licking his Lips
my message not understood
Moody Miss, you Must Make up your Mind
before this trickle's a flood
So Shall we Share the Shortbread, Shirley?

Surely She Should!

Shall we share the shortbread, Shirley?
Surely we should!
There's only one piece left
and like to eat it we both would
But, hang on, Shirley – look at the shortbread –
it's caked in mud

(Mud?? Well, it seemed to be...)

Shirley shivered and shrieked "You can shove it!"

And greedy guts giggled, "Oh, good!"

(But it wasn't mud. While Shirley wasn't looking, I'd smeared some potted meat on from an abandoned sandwich. Boy, it tasted good... like a traditional sweetmeat – mmm, lovely!)

Shall we share the shortbread, Shirley ? Surely
we should...

(But, yes, I took the biscuit! Yum Yum!)

Northern Pictures in association with Chic Ken Productions presents the world film premiere of...

John Shuttleworth

in

SOUTHERN SOFTIES

26. Food Cupboard Shuffle Day

Once a month my wife Mary likes to go through all the items in the food cupboard, moving any with a short date to the front for immediate consumption and relocating those items which boast a long date (and therefore longer shelf life) to the back of the cupboard. It's a responsible job but also a fun task, and for many years I've joined her in doing it. But, just lately, Mary has preferred to do the job alone. Am I crestfallen about that? Yes and no – I'm philosophical about it, and totally understand Mary's reasons. "You do?" (I hear you cry). Yes, I do! (I reply). "Well, let's hear the reasons, John!" (I hear you continue). Yes, you're about to (I conclude, even though I've barely started!).

You see, readers, only a few years ago I was in the hallowed position of being allowed to help Mary with the job of moving foodstuffs into the correct position based on their shelf life. But one day something happened which shattered Mary's confidence in me undertaking this simple task. This chapter is all about that fateful day. I'm tempted to say the story is "hard-hitting from the outset" (like the programmes Mary likes to watch on telly), but it's not really. It *is* perturbing at times, definitely, and yet at times, I hope, heartwarming too.

It began as a normal 'Food Cupboard Shuffle Day', as I like to call it. Under Mary's watchful and expert eye, I had already moved a jar of crab paste (short date) from the back to the front and a tin of chickpeas in water (long date) to the back of the shelf. I've no idea where those chickpeas came from, to be honest. They might have been left by our Karen when she came to visit last, but they're not the sort of thing we tend to enjoy. I'm sure some of you will have thought that as soon as I said 'chickpeas'. And I agree – it's not the sort of product I relish having on the premises. Relish? Oof, I bet you're thinking about that now, aren't you? Me too, but don't worry – all the sauces and relishes are in the fridge. Hang on – apart from one bottle of unopened ketchup which has a very long date so will be stood not too far away from where those blinking chickpeas were moved to.

I'd just relocated a tin of luncheon meat (medium expiry date) from the back of the shelf to a central position when I heard Mary let out a loud groan. What was going on? Well, unbeknownst to me, she'd taken the jar of crab paste from the shelf and had been studying it, then before I knew what was happening, had angrily flung the jar into the pedal bin. (Incidentally, we used to have a big shiny chrome bin, like they have at the hairdressers, but we just couldn't get on with it. The problem was you could see yourself approaching in it, and although initially we loved that convenience, ultimately we found it disconcerting, so we went back to the small pedal bin.) Sorry, back to the story, which I'm sure you'll agree is suddenly hotting up!

I gasped audibly at Mary's violent act and asked her what the heck she was doing throwing the crab paste away – a product I had already checked and certified as a 'front of shelf' item. Mary gave me a horrified stare and said, "You nearly killed us, John!" and with that left the room in disgust. What could have happened? I dived into the bin to recover the little jar (and let's face it, they are little, aren't they? Those crab and salmon jars, ridiculously so) to read the expiry date. I expected that I must have completely misread it and that instead of April 2024 it was October 2013 or something. But, no, I'd been right... 'Best Before April 24' it said as clear as day. So what was the problem? Had Mary lost her marbles? Did she think it was now 2035 or something?

But then, suddenly, I clocked what Mary had spotted – a tiny but crucial detail that my initial examination had totally missed: the seal on the jar had already been broken! A quick twist of the tiny lid (well, it would be a tiny lid screwing onto a tiny jar!) confirmed this and revealed inside a thick layer of white wooly mould (covering half a jarful of rancid and foul-smelling crab paste). Disgusting! And I blame our son Darren for this. He must have opened the jar several months previously and used some of it for a sandwich when he popped round for his tea as he does sometimes (prior to leaving for his evening shift working at the off-licence). And then, instead of putting the jar in the fridge – to be consumed within the next day or two – had placed it back on the food cupboard shelf.

Being so tiny the jar had remained unspotted for weeks and even months, hidden perhaps behind a jar of 'pestio' (that green stuff our Karen likes which, ironically, *does* resemble mould!) So, although its 'Use By' date was – as stated on the jar – still a few weeks away, clearly it wasn't fit for human consumption. Perhaps it was her long experience working as a dinner lady at a local primary school or just a mother's instinct, but my wife, Mary Shuttleworth, had been totally on the ball, while my judgement and ability to perform unsupervised on 'Food Cupboard Shuffle Day' had been found wanting. Certainly, I could never be trusted again by Mary. "NEVER EVER!" Mary said at the time as she stormed out of the room. Oof, that was a bit harsh, don't you think, readers?

Stop Press: having said all that, Mary has recently hinted that it might not be 'never ever'. By her own admission, she finds 'Food Cupboard Shuffle Day' a bit boring and she knows how much I like it. So one day soon, she says I might be let loose again on FCSD! Hoo-oo, exciting! And yet, if Mary were ever to learn of my terrible secret, I don't think she'd be considering welcoming me back. "What secret, John?" (you may be wondering). "You kept that quiet!" Well, of course I did – it's a secret! (I reply with a wink!).

Let me explain by taking you back to the moment when I realised I'd cocked up by not noticing the broken seal.

Back in the bin went the mouldy crab paste, but before the bin lid could close (yes, it has a soft close mechanism, just like our toilet seat) I saw something familiar inside the bin, a face I recognised, and I'm sure you would have too, readers, had you been looking into our bin at that moment. It was the happy smiling face of legendary TV chef Ainsley Harriott. Not in the bin itself – he's a big lad, and although he might have just about fitted into our large chrome bin, no way could he have squeezed into our pedal bin. I saw Ainsley's face on the front of a box of one of his excellent soups. I say excellent, but I've never tried them. The flavour of this one was 'Aromatic Thai Chicken and Lemongrass'. Oof, I don't know your thoughts about that flavour, but to me it sounds way too exotic for the UK market, and – I hope I'm wrong here, but – might it not contain ingredients that border on 'illegal'? I hope I'm wrong, I really do, but anyhow, let it be known that in all other respects I'm a huge fan of the irrepressible Mr Harriott, and so it was distressing to see him grinning up at me from deep inside the bin.

Mary must have put the packet in there while I was enjoying a short comfort break only minutes before. I lifted poor Ainsley (the soup packet) out of the bin to check just how many weeks out of date he was. I couldn't believe it – still 'in date' for three more days! What on earth was Mary thinking of? I turned to tell her off, but, of course, she wasn't there. Perhaps she'd nipped into our garage to assess how many tins of vegetables remained in the 'Overflow Canned Vegetables Section', which is another name I've made up, although I don't think it's quite as catchy as 'Food Cupboard Shuffle Day', do you, readers? Or maybe she'd nipped upstairs with her fresh ironing and then sat on the bed to have a little weep about my foolhardy behaviour – oof, hopefully not. But it was good that she wasn't there as I had hatched a devious plan!

First, I wiped the Ainsley soup box down thoroughly with a dishcloth (primed with anti-bacterial spray), then placed it carefully at the front of the food cupboard. Mary wouldn't be happy seeing a product that she'd just got rid of reinstated. But Ainsley's soup wasn't mouldy – it was still in date, and although the flavour may be overly exotic for mine or Mary's tastes, surely the soup deserved its time at the front of the food cupboard? Yes, it would only be three days, but that's 72 hours, you know, which is quite a long time really.

Then I thought again: even though the front of the shelf was his rightful location, I realised Ainsley *had* to be hidden from Mary's gaze, or back in the bin he would surely go as soon as the cupboard door was opened and she clocked him. She was in a bad mood already, remember, after I'd nearly killed us with the mouldy crab paste, so would be in no mood for compromise. So I moved Ainsley to the back of the shelf, next to the weird chickpeas (sorry, Ainsley!) and other foodstuffs with long dates. I started to close the cupboard door, then realised I could still see Ainsley's face at the back of the shelf. Normally, it's the gloomy part of the cupboard, but Ainsley's big cheery grin seemed to be lighting it up.

At that moment, I heard the tell-tale pad of Mary's slippers on the stairs – I needed to move fast. While I was loath to totally conceal the soup packet, in his current position Ainsley was vulnerable to detection. What should I do? I heard the sound of Mary's slippers change from the 'pad' on carpet to the 'slap' of slipper on kitchen lino. Oof! I quickly turned Ainsley round 180 degrees, but that wasn't going to work. There was another photo of him on the back grinning just as much as on the front. I had a mere second to conceal Ainsley with a box of sage and onion stuffing mix before Mary appeared. Phew, I managed it, and it was comforting to realise that Ainsley would be safe there until Christmas at least!

As it happens, we had a posh 'chestnut' stuffing mix at Christmas, so the sage and onion one is still there, and as far as I know Ainsley is there too – still smiling – at the back of our cupboard. And he's smiling on the telly too, of course – he was on the other night grinning away. That soup sachet is heavily out of date now, and as 'Food Cupboard Shuffle Day' approaches once more I know it's only a matter of time before Ainsley has to leave us and that grin will disappear from our cupboard for ever. Unless… we buy another packet of his soups. Perhaps the 'Cream of Wild Mushroom' flavour? Oof, Ainsley, why did you have to insert the word 'wild' in it? Why can't you just do a plain 'Cream of Tomato' or 'Oxtail'!

Oof, that was a story and half, wasn't it, readers? It's hard to determine whether it's got a happy ending? Let's give it one by finishing with a song that celebrates not just

Ainsley Harriott's winning smile but the smile in general. It's a rare song of mine – to date it's only been performed in my travel documentary *It's Nice Up North* set in the Shetland Islands. The movie was filmed by internationally renowned stills photographer Martin Parr. Incredibly, despite his international renown, Martin doesn't do weddings, or take portraits of kittens in a basket, which is not only a missed opportunity but something which makes you totally question Martin's photographic credentials. He's a super bloke though, with a lovely smile to rival even Ainsley's!

You're Not Fully Dressed Unless You're Wearing a Smile

You're not fully dressed unless you're wearing a smile
So put one on – let everyone admire your style
If you're looking sad
(I'm talking to you, lad!)
If you're not looking glad
Then you're only partially clad
You're not fully dressed unless you're wearing a smile

You're not fully dressed unless you're sporting a grin
So take off that sad expression and chuck it in the bin
While you're looking glum
(Are you listening to me, chum?)
While you're looking glum
You are showing 'builder's bum'
Oh, you're not fully dressed unless you're wearing a smile

No, you're not fully dressed unless you're wearing a smile!

27. Getting Heated Over the Fridge

A clever title, I'm sure you'll agree. But there's nothing clever about the marital friction that fridge temperature disagreements can cause, I assure you. You could argue this chapter should have been included in my previous book, *Two Margarines and Other Domestic Dilemmas* (still available at all good charity shops and even brand new at some good bookshops, plus online at www.shuttleworths.co.uk), and it would have been, if I'd thought of it before now.

Getting heated over the fridge is what was happening for many years in our house. That's because my wife Mary and I would keep telling each other off for changing the temperature and then defiantly change it back in front of the other person, causing deep upset. For instance, I'd turn it down and then Mary would turn it up again, only for me to turn it down again even before Mary's back was turned. It was a dangerous practice – I was playing with fire and, boy, did I know it!

However, a few years ago, I began turning the dial

down just slightly, without Mary's knowledge, and then a few days later I'd turn it down another notch, and it was gratifying to note that my action would go unspotted for ages. But then I realised Mary was doing exactly the same thing – changing the temperature when I was out performing at the drop-in centre, for instance – and her sneakiness would also go undetected for some considerable time.

You see, Mary likes it set at three and a half (four or even more over the Yuletide period, which is crazy given that that's a time when it's colder and the snow is lying 'deep and crisp and even'). I, on the other hand, fervently believe that two or even one and a half is a perfectly adequate temperature for a fridge all year round. So after years of disagreeing about the perfect fridge temperature, nowadays life is harmonious thanks to 'Secret Temperature Changing' or STC for short. Oof, I've created an 'anchorman' as I believe it's called, or is it 'ancronhymn'? (If so, that doesn't sound as good as 'anchorman', does it?) But, yes, by employing the STC system and not alerting the other person to the fact that the fridge temperature has been changed, neither of us seem to notice for days or even weeks. And by the time we do find out, we feel a bit foolish that we didn't notice immediately, so to get angry seems inappropriate. (To be fair, Mary can still get a bit waspish when she finds out!) But generally nothing is said. We simply readjust the thermostat to the temperature we believe is the correct one and then go about our daily lives, safe in the knowledge that with any luck we'll have a week or two with the fridge at a temperature we like. So, readers… if you're constantly falling out with your loved one over fridge temperatures, why don't you try mine and Mary's marvellous method? (Oof, there were too many words beginning with 'm' there, weren't there, readers? Apologies!)

I realise I've made the STC system sound easy, but beware… there are pitfalls. For instance, when you plan to change the temperature you must first establish that you're alone in the kitchen and unlikely to be disturbed. You don't want your partner to catch you red-handed (blue-handed would be more accurate in my case because the fridge is so blinking cold at three and a half!). Concentrate as you change the temperature wheel to the desired temperature (ideally two). And you *do* have to concentrate: don't be cocky and think you can do it while getting out a big carton of orange juice at the same time or you'll come a cropper – dropping the orange juice and inadvertently setting the temperature too high or too low. Think of it like you're opening a safe and you've got to get the right combination. Bend your knees slightly if that helps.

Once you've changed the temperature to two (notice the clever and subtle way I'm encouraging you to set the fridge to two by continually repeating the number two), you may be surprised how long it is before your handiwork is detected. Weeks, even months sometimes. I can't pretend I don't cut myself a small, satisfied chuckle if Mary hasn't noticed and it's still at two after a fortnight, and you should feel free to do the same. But, again, beware! I once gave an audible chuckle, and Mary, who was nearby at the kitchen table preparing vegetables for a family meal, said, "What's happening in the fridge that's so amusing then?" Now, if there'd been a misshapen vegetable in the fridge I would have been able to blame my mirth on seeing that, like Esther Rantzen used to on *That's Life*. But Mary had all the vegetables with her on the table and, regrettably, there was nothing amusing about any of their shapes. So how could I explain my involuntary guffaw? I looked around the fridge for things that might provoke laughter. The pickled onion jar was nearly empty with just one pickled onion remaining, but what's funny about that? If anything, that's quite sad. If there had been 'two margarines on the go', then that would have been worthy of comment. But not a chuckle – a big sigh more like, or a tut. I was struggling to think of anything to say to Mary to allay her suspicion and, as my silence continued, I knew it was only going to be a matter of time before she put down her paring knife, got up from the table and came to look for herself, and then she'd notice the fridge's temperature was two. And then marital misery would ensue!

Can you guess what I did, readers? I can't believe you will because it was surely the most stupid thing a person fully in charge of his faculties has ever done! I panicked and changed the temperature from two (where it had happily been for weeks) back to three and a half (Mary's Arctic temperature!) and hurriedly closed the fridge door, saying nothing. Meanwhile, Mary had become distracted by a potato with several eyes in it and had forgotten all about my chuckle. Oh, what a fool I'd been. I needn't have changed the temperature, but I had done and now I was faced with the challenge of having to change the temperature back to two without Mary noticing. The close shave with disaster had knocked my confidence, however, so I didn't do it straight away. I decided to leave it at three and a half for a while – at least until after we'd had our tea.

After tea, we relocated to the lounge to watch telly as normal. I decided the best plan would be to slip back into the kitchen on the pretext of loading the dishwasher, while Mary remained in the lounge watching a forensic crime documentary (hard-hitting from the outset!). While in the kitchen I would open the fridge door and do an STC without Mary knowing. A simple plan and surely foolproof.

However, I started watching the programme with her, and it was so hard-hitting that I forgot all about my mission in the kitchen. Bedtime was fast approaching, and when it was time to heat up the milk for my hot chocolate, I was tired and my reaction times had become slow. Mentally, I felt sluggish – I decided it was simply too risky to try to change the temperature that evening with Mary still hovering on the ground floor.

The following day I forgot all about the fridge temperature as I decided to visit the Brough Rest Area on the A46 near Newark, and last-minute preparations were all-consuming. This included filling two separate drinks flasks – one with leaf tea and the other with golden vegetable soup (no croutons). In the days immediately after my day trip (and we'll be hearing all about that very shortly!) I had more distracting tasks to execute – scraping some moss from our drain cover and undenting a ping pong ball by warming it with boiling water, jobs like that which prevented me from focusing on the task of resetting the fridge temperature to two. Before I knew it, it was time to prepare for my weekly trip with Ken Worthington to check the level of the Ladybower Reservoir. A new bag of travel mints had to be placed in the glove compartment of my Austin Ambassador, plus a sachet of handy wipes.

So, unfortunately, the fridge remained at three and a half for around a week, I reckon. I don't really remember – it was a good few years ago when all this happened. It got changed back to two eventually, I'm sure. Anyway, I'm bored now of discussing the temperature of the fridge. Fascinating as it is, I'd like to end this chapter with a song all about my trip to the Brough Rest Area, which I was extremely fired up about at the time. Although all did not go to plan, as you will now hear…

The Brough Rest Area

Looking back, I should have been warier
Getting excited by a mere road sign
But when I saw it – the Brough Rest Area –
Little shivers ran down my spine

Have you heard of the Brough Rest Area?
It's near Newark on the A46
I saw the sign and said, "Oo, look, Mary, a
place where we can stretch our legs."

(Although we didn't bother because we'd had a stop at a
Jet garage only minutes earlier.)

Brough Rest Area, what could be merrier?
I envisaged an idyllic scene
Sipping lemonade in a shady glade
Children paddling a stream

I planned a trip to the Brough Rest Area
Invited Mary, she said, "Go on your own!"
I planned to arrive mid-morning and tarry there
till the warden said, "Oy, you! Go home!"

The great day came at last, I'd prepared a flask
Though no doubt there would be a catering van
I saw the sign appear, let out a cheer

"Yippee aye ay, here I am!"

Here I am at the Brough Rest Area
But I have sad news, my friends
All there is at the Brough Rest Area
Is a lay-by and two wheelie bins

(Great news, readers! As I write, there are now six permanent bins in the lay-by – three on each side of the A46. Clearly, things are looking up for the Brough Rest Area! But I have to say, as a picnic destination it's no substitute for Wyming Brook or the Toad Mouth Rock near Hathersage.)

RBM presents

out of our sheds

JOHN* SHUTTLEWORTH

"WONDERFUL, WACKY AND WEIRD"

RADIO TIMES

THE GUARDIAN

9.40pm

13-20 August

8 SHOWS ONLY!

23 PLEASANCE DOME

0131 556 6550 pleasance.co.uk

www.shuttleworths.co.uk twitter@johnshuttlewrth

photo: Tony Briggs, design: Steve Ullathorne

28. Unaccompanied Lady

SO I PUT DOWN MY FACTPACK AND TIPTOED OUT TO THE GENTS FOR A QUICK SPLASHDOWN.

THEN I POPPED TO THE BAR
FOR AN ORANGE JUICE
AND I SAW AS I SAT DOWN...

...AN UNACCOMPANIED LADY
SITTING AT THE BAR.
UNACCOMPANIED LADY
I WONDER WHO YOU ARE.

..HER STOOP TO RETRIEVE A PACKET OF NUTS SHE'D DROPPED UPON THE FLOOR.

OH, UNACCOMPANIED LADY
SITTING AT THE BAR.

UNACCOMPANIED LADY,
I WONDER WHO YOU ARE.

AT THAT MOMENT
A MAN APPEARED –
HER HUSBAND,
I PRESUME.

DAVE
WINTERBOTTOM
BAKEWELL DIVISION

E KISSED HER AND BRISKLY WHISKED HER AWAY
ACK TO THE CONFERENCE ROOM.
DENISE
I SAW THEM LATER IN THE CARVERY
SHARING A LEG OF LAMB...

AND CURSED MYSELF FOR FORGETTING BRIEFLY THAT I'M A MARRIED MAN!

OH, UNACCOMPANIED LADY,
SITTING AT THE BAR.
UNACCOMPANIED LADY,
I WONDER WHERE YOU ARE...?

RBM PRESENTS
'The 42nd best reason to love Britain'
SUNDAY TELEGRAPH
JOHN
SHUTTLEWORTH
A Wee Ken To Remember
TOUR 2014
TICKETS & INFORMATION FROM: www.shuttleworths.co.uk @johnshuttlewrth
www.rbmcomedy.com

29. Stay at Home and Protect the VHS

Note: this chapter deals head on with all the mental ills of the world, and once you've read it, even the maddest person will be back to normal.

Another note: Please remember I'm not medically qualified to say that so I could be very wide of the mark in my supposition. You know, don't blame me if this chapter pushes you over the edge – but I honestly don't think it will.

Firstly, 'How's your mental health?' Until recently, it was considered rather rude to ask people that question. Nowadays, it seems rude *not* to ask it. Having said that, don't ask it too often of the same person or they might start to get a bit paranoid and anxious, and that might lead to, erm… mental health problems. This happened to my dear friend Ken Worthington during the lockdown. As you may know, Ken is a single gentleman who lives alone (unlike myself, surrounded by supportive family members – well, my wife Mary), and the isolation he endured on a daily basis made me – during the pandemic – extremely concerned for his wellbeing.

So, for several months back in 2020, I asked Ken every day how his mental health was. Sometimes by telephone, other times in person by calling round to his house – often late at night (when I feared he might be most vulnerable). Once I even sent Ken a greeting card with a photo of a meerkat on, because they're quite anxious-looking creatures, aren't they, and you suspect their mental health might not be too good. (Like those llamas that have loonies talking to them all day long!) Well, you'd think Ken would have been grateful for my interventions and that regular contact with a concerned neighbour would have kept him on an even keel, but it seemed to have the opposite effect. He became surly and diffident, avoiding eye contact and sometimes even refusing to open the door to me. I'd hear him cursing and even moaning behind the door and naturally I became concerned for his sanity. Some of you might insist I should have notified the authorities at that point and had him sectioned, but I didn't want the responsibility of having to water his plants while he was away from his property (they all seem to need different amounts of watering, don't they, and I'd worry that I'd get it wrong, you see). So, eventually, I just left him to it.

The thing is, readers, I *did* have cause to doubt his sanity during the lockdown because I discovered he'd started baking his own bread, which is a bit nutty in itself, in't it? I told Ken he should be buying a small Warburton's twice a week or even placing a regular order with the local baker and having a soothing conversation with them during the transaction. But Ken ignored my advice and carried on home baking. And then I heard something which really disturbed me – Ken had begun making bread using dough that was sour. Ugh, it's dirty to do that, isn't it, and Ken was clearly now losing his grip on reality.

If you don't want to make someone depressed by continually asking how their mental health is, what *can* you do? I suggest you try just chatting to them about anything in a cordial manner, as that can help maintain their mental stability. "Yes, I'm sure it does," I hear you cry, "but what happens if you've got nothing to talk to them about?" Very good question – and this is exactly what happened with Ken and me during the lockdown (after I'd contacted him again and apologised for destroying his mental health with my continual questioning). You see, we had absolutely nothing to discuss. Not even the weather because that late springtime it was lovely and sunny every day, do you remember? So, after a few days, the weather wasn't even worth mentioning.

Nor could we discuss professional matters, because during lockdown I had no upcoming shows at the drop-in centre or hospice. Ordinarily, Ken passes on useful information to me, such as where to plug in my organ, the bay number of my allocated parking space, etc. A versatile singer/organist like me needs help and guidance on big decisions like that and I'm so lucky to have a wily old pro like Ken, ready to dispense this information swiftly, accurately and with a big dollop of friendly reassurance; unless he doesn't know what's happening, and then he looks wide-eyed and starts shaking, and saliva appears at the side of his mouth. But, thanks, Ken – oh, what times we had! And hopefully there's a few more engagements in the pipeline, Kenny boy? (That's a subtle hint to Ken as I have to say currently bookings are a bit thin on the ground!)

So… with the weather and business matters both off the menu, the only other topics that might hold Ken's attention would be drinking (Malibu) and going for a curry, as these are Ken's two biggest passions. But they're not mine, I'm afraid. As you may or may not know, I don't like curry, apart from the 'pompidom', and I prefer bashing them with my fist to see them shatter into many pieces rather than actually eating them. As for alcohol – I enjoy a schooner of sherry at Whitsuntide, and that's it. Tell a lie, I had some red wine one Christmas and, as I mentioned earlier, it *is* like drinking blood, isn't it? Alan the Opera Singer's wife Pauline told me that once; she whispered it to me as she was leaving our house after visiting with Alan in the early nineties, and I didn't believe her, but Pauline's words stayed in my mind, and years later as I drank this red wine that's all I could think of. "Ugh, I'm drinking blood!" Oh dear, I hope that thought hasn't invaded your subconscious. If it has, and you happen to be cracking open a bottle of red wine in the near future – and I suspect that's quite a few of you – well, you'll be in trouble. There'll be a lot left in the bottle. You might even find yourselves tipping it down the sink. Apologies if that's the case, because I know it's quite pricey, but blame Alan the Opera Singer's wife Pauline as the 'blood' idea came from her!

Note: if you're feeling anaemic, for goodness' sake don't start injecting yourself with red wine!

So what *could* Ken and I talk about? The answer is – NOTHING! We'd sit in silence and a good few metres apart, even though we didn't have to as Ken was in my bubble. It was a sorry state of affairs, and after a while I stopped hanging out with him and soon it was *my* mental health that was affected because Mary had gone back to work as a dinner lady at the local primary school so I was on my own too much – I was lonely. My salvation came suddenly – not by baking bread but, wait for it, writing poetry! That's right: it used to be that if you were quite snooty with a cravat and silk breeches you wrote poems, didn't it? Not any more. Hardened lifers in prison write poetry nowadays, so I've been told, and I believe a lot of ordinary folks did so during the pandemic. I did too. Well, I only wrote one poem, and it's very short, and I hesitate to share it with you in case you think it's rubbish or – more worryingly – tell the police about it and they arrest me. Mind you, if I went to jail, then, of course, I could write more poetry in the prison (as long as paper and pen could be smuggled in)! But read the poem and you'll soon realise that what appears to be wilful lawbreaking is really me being a loving husband – staying at home and obeying lockdown rules.

Flaunting the Lockdown

I was not down
During the lockdown
Though no one popped round
I flaunted the lockdown
I went to the garden centre
Well, I stood by the washing-line pole
(Which is bang centre of our garden, you see!)
I admired a local beauty spot
Well, I peered at Mary's mole!

Do you get it? Quite clever, in't it? And notice how some of the poem doesn't rhyme, because you're not supposed to do rhyming any more, in poetry, Ken says. I just did a little bit at the end, because I can't help rhyming, being a top song-lyric writer!

Another way to improve your mental health is by doing a jigsaw. Or is it? Personally, I wouldn't, as – unless it's a really easy jigsaw aimed at young kiddies – it'll drive you crackers, and you might get so frustrated with not being able to do it, you'll flip the board into the air with an anguished cry, scattering the pieces everywhere, which is really awful behaviour. Please don't do that; you'll make yourself no friends doing things like that. And you'll have to get on your hands and knees to laboriously pick up all those little pieces – a depressing activity which could cause your mental health to plummet further!

An activity which you'd assume is relaxing and

improves mental health is ping pong – or 'table tennis' as it's known by accomplished players like me. (I was lucky enough to have had formal coaching every Wednesday evening at the YMCA back in the seventies, which is where I met my future wife, Mary, who was also being coached.) The quality of your opponent really does determine the level of your enjoyment. If I play Mary – a rare occurrence these days as the rubber on her bat has perished, causing her to lose confidence – then I have a lovely time and am reminded of why we're still together. Because Mary is attacking with top spin shots and I'm defensive with the hard bat doing back hand spin. It's a recipe for a long rally (and long relationship), which is exactly what Mary and I have enjoyed for many years now.

However, if you're playing against someone who's rubbish like Ken Worthington, then it's the most depressing activity known to man. Ken continually hits the ball too high or off at a wild angle, missing the table by miles. As his opponent your main job becomes not playing table tennis, not even playing 'ping pong', but searching for the blinking ball, often on hands and knees, trying to fish it out from underneath chairs or from behind the radiator. Then, once you've retrieved it, returned to the table and resumed the game, seconds later he's hit it behind you again and you're doing exactly the same thing. It's totally dispiriting and creates not just ill feeling but dreadful wear and tear on your joints. And all the time you're bending down, Ken is laughing his head off, acting like it's all a big joke. Well, it's not, it's a *very* unpleasant experience!

What if you do find that a difficult jigsaw or a game of ping pong against a poor opponent has sent you into a spiral of despair? Is there a remedy? Well, how about doing some gambling? Before you say “I beg your pardon, Mr Shuttleworth! Gambling – good for mental health?”, let me just remind you that some of the happiest, most life-affirming adverts on the telly are for gambling, haven’t you noticed? Those ads make gambling look a lot of fun – dozens of happy people singing and dancing in the street, fantastic! So go on, have a flutter! Oof, no, that’s a crazy idea! You’ll lose all your hard-earned money! Then again, if you gamble responsibly and only lose what you can afford to win (or something like that they say, don’t they?), then you should be fine.

Next time me and Mary go to Sutton-on-Sea to check on Ken’s chalet – and that might be sooner than you realise, keep reading, folks! – we might pop to nearby Mablethorpe and the Amusement Arcade to have a flutter on the Penny Falls. The important thing is to enjoy gambling with your mates or the rest of the family, so I’ll give Mary 40 to 50 pee’s worth of two pence pieces so she can have a go too. (Though if she wins, I will expect her to reimburse me to the tune of her original stake.) It’s when you gamble alone and the stakes get too high, that’s when your mental health can plummet. So stick to the machines that take two pence pieces. Don’t get cocky and play the ten pence machines, unless you’re totally confident and there’s a big happy group around you – to buoy up your spirits when you lose that ten pee, which you probably will do!

If the gambling becomes uncontrollable and – God forbid – you start putting £1 pieces in the fruit machines (just think how many doughnuts or sticks of candyfloss you could have bought instead!), then your family may well reject you, and the happy crowd in the street will turn down a side road, leaving you all alone, depressed and isolated, and this is where Alexa might be a lifesaver. You know, those cylindrical machines with a spinning blue ring that you can talk to. You say "Alexa, what shall I do today?" and she suggests interesting options. Ken Worthington has one, and during the lockdown he was feeling quite artistic, so one day he said, "Alexa, what shall I draw?" Well, Ken was expecting a sensible reply like "A nice bowl of cherries, Ken, and don't forget to sharpen your pencil first!" Nothing could have prepared Ken for the bizarre reply he *did* receive. "Draw something really deep like an abyss," said Alexa. What a strange suggestion, and for an emotionally fragile man such as Ken, a dangerous one!

He thought Alexa might have misunderstood, so he asked again. "Alexa, what should I draw?" The reply was as strange as the first time. "Draw what wind would look like if you could see it." That's crazy, and irresponsible, and it's going to use up a lot of lead in your pencil doing swirly patterns. And I question the airy-fairy nature of Alexa's bizarre suggestion. How long would Ken have to keep asking to get the bowl of cherries? He decided to ask one more time. "Alexa, what should I draw?" The answer Ken received was the most disturbing yet. "Imagine gravity has stopped working in your house and draw that!"

Needless to say, Ken didn't attempt any sketches that day. He unplugged his Alexa and went for a lie down. He was a nervous wreck. I don't know who programmes these computers, but I suggest they might be run not by AI but AS (Artificial Stupidity!). Either that or Alexa is partial to the wacky baccy (as I believe it's known).

Writing poetry, baking bread, drawing, doing jigsaws and playing ping pong… as well as not guaranteeing mental health improvement, all have the drawback of requiring use of your hands. Wouldn't you rather indulge in an activity which improves mental wellbeing but allows your hands to be free to unwrap a toffee while you scratch your tummy? It sounds too good to be true, doesn't it, but it's achievable. Just sit down on the sofa and watch TV for a while. It doesn't have to be a programme that's hard-hitting and with strong language from the outset. In fact, it's preferable if it isn't. But as most of live telly these days is like that, I suggest you dig out your old video tapes of classic dramas and put one on. Even if it's not raining, my advice is:

Stay at Home and Protect the VHS

You may be wondering what your video player's
for
It's a possession you tend to ignore
It fills a gap between the telly and the floor
But you don't use it any more

Oh, what a shame, please try to recollect
The thrill you felt when you first spied that deck
Heard the clunk and whirr as the tape slid in the
slot.
And now you want to chuck it – better not!

Stay at home and protect the VHS
If you don't, you'll have one VHS less
How important it is I cannot stress
To stay at home and protect the VHS

So find that episode of *Bergerac* you taped
Off the TV back in 1988
Enjoy the muffled sound
And the fuzzy picture too
Then watch a *Lovejoy*
Maybe watch two

DVD is not for me – save the VHS

Blu-ray no way – save the VHS
Can't relax with Betamax though some say it was best
Stay at home and protect the VHS

Stay at home and protect the VHS
If you don't, you'll have one VHS less
How important it is I cannot stress
To stay at home and protect the VHS

RBM PRESENTS
'THE GODFATHER OF CHARACTER COMEDY' EVENING STANDARD
JOHN SHUTTLEWORTH
My Last Will & Tasty Mint
UK TOUR 2017
JANUARY 2017
11 SWINDON Arts Centre (PREVIEW)
12 READING South St (PREVIEW)
13 STAMFORD Arts Centre (PREVIEW)
16 BARTON ON HUMBER Ropewalk (PREVIEW)
18 LEEDS City Varieties
19 LEEDS City Varieties
20 NEWCASTLE Tyne Theatre
21 LIVERPOOL Playhouse
25 SALFORD Lowry
26 SALFORD Lowry
27 CHELMSFORD Civic Theatre
28 MARGATE Theatre Royal
29 MILTON KEYNES Stables
FEBRUARY 2017
01 NOTTINGHAM Playhouse
02 CHELTENHAM Town Hall
03 SWANSEA Pontadarwe Arts Centre
04 PORTSMOUTH Theatre Royal
07 BRIGHTON The Old Market
08 EXETER Phoenix
09 WIMBORNE Tivoli
10 LINCOLN Drill Hall
12 BIRMINGHAM Town Hall
13 BUXTON Opera House
15 LEICESTER Little Theatre
17 BRISTOL Old Vic
18 WAKEFIELD Theatre Royal
21 LONDON Leicester Square Theatre
22 LONDON Leicester Square Theatre
23 LONDON Leicester Square Theatre
24 STRATFORD UPON AVON Arts House
26 SCUNTHORPE Plowright
27 ILKLEY Kings Hall
28 SCARBOROUGH Stephen Joseph Theatre
MARCH 2017
13 BEVERLEY East Riding Theatre
15 NORWICH Playhouse
18 MANCHESTER Dancehouse
19 MANCHESTER Dancehouse
21 HEBDEN BRIDGE Picture House
22 LANCASTER Grand Theatre
23 GLASGOW Citizens Theatre
24 EDINBURGH Queens Hall
30 SHEFFIELD City Hall
'HIS MUSIC ISN'T JUST MUSIC ...IT'S AURAL PROZAC' THE INDEPENDENT
TICKETS & INFORMATION FROM:
www.shuttleworths.co.uk
@johnshuttlewrth www.rbmcomedy.com

30.
A Day Trip to Mablethorpe

I know what you're thinking: "You're crazy to undertake such a big journey in just one day, especially in an elderly motor car like an Austin Ambassador Y Reg." Well, you're not wrong, my friend. To drive all the way from Sheffield, South Yorkshire, to the seaside town of Mablethorpe in Lincolnshire and back without an overnight stay may be regarded as foolhardy. But my wife Mary and I need to be back before nightfall. "Why's that then?" you may enquire. "To prepare some potato wedges prior to shoving them in the air fryer?" Ooh, I hadn't thought of that, but it sounds delicious and I'd love to… if only we had an air fryer. Our Darren and his fiancée Jasmin have one, but Mary and I are still waiting for prices to tumble sufficiently before taking the plunge. It feels like the same rollercoaster emotional journey we embarked on in the late eighties as we waited for microwave oven prices to tumble. Eventually they did, and it was a fabulous day when we went to Laskys and bought one. Sadly, that microwave has long gone and so too has Laskys!

But Mablethorpe is still there. In fact, it's thriving. The town is famous for having a Ghost Train that only costs 50 pee a ride! Well, that was the fare when I was last there, around, oo, erm… it was the mid nineties I reckon, so I suppose it might be a pound or even £1.50 by now. Oof, that's a bit pricey! The doughnuts were very nice, as I recall – packed with nourishing goodness. And in Mablethorpe an expansive beach of white sand greets the lucky visitor.

But to answer your question, Mary and I like to be back home at a reasonable hour to prep the veg ready for the evening meal. There may be additional tasks that I personally will be responsible for, like setting up the ironing board in the lounge (if Mary plans to iron as she views *The Chase* or a hard-hitting drama after our evening meal), and in anticipation of that eventuality, I like to check the TV remote: verifying that all the buttons are working smoothly, taking out and reinserting the triple A batteries in case there's a dicky contact, and even replacing the batteries if necessary. Can you see now why it's only a day trip to Mablethorpe?

So let's get going! Oof, we can't – we're waiting for Mary and Joan Chitty, who will be Mary's companion on the seaside jaunt.

"Mary? Joan? Hurry up, please!"

I've just tooted the horn as well – a very short toot, as I'm mindful I'm in a stationary vehicle and the sounding of a horn is highly illegal. "No Ken Worthington today?" you may ask, keen that I too should have a companion as I stroll along the seafront. Ken was invited but declined as he has a lot of office paperwork to catch up on. But I think we'll cope without him. In fact, he'd have been a blinking nuisance. You see, my main mission in travelling to Mablethorpe is to make a brief stop at the neighbouring village of Sutton-on-Sea where Ken has a holiday chalet. While Mary and Joan stroll on the beach (or round the Pound Shop) I shall be checking the chalet lock and examining the door and windows to check for damage and any evidence of water ingress. These are delicate jobs best done without a man with a bubble perm shrieking excitedly how happy he is to be back in his holiday home.

I also have a full bag of Werther's Originals to keep me company. And they will surely be needed, for part of our journey will take me on one of the most boring roads in the UK (so I've been told) – the M180. Sucking on a Werther's will surely help me concentrate and prevent me nodding off or wandering onto the hard shoulder – oof, not that I'd ever do that, readers!

Incidentally, please do come along. I anticipate the two ladies will elect to sit on the back seat of my Y Reg, which I always like. It makes me feel like I'm a taxi driver – one of those that take you to the airport. This means I have an empty front passenger seat, so why not hop in and make yourself comfortable as we wait for the ladies?

"Mary! Joan! We need to hit the road… oo, I say!"

"John…. wait for me!"

Oof, you'll never guess who has just appeared in our driveway… It's next-door neighbour and sole agent Ken Worthington!

"I thought you said you weren't coming, Ken."

"I wasn't, but I've just finished some very tedious paperwork and now I'd like a trip to the seaside. Besides, I'd rather check my own chalet for once! Is that alright?"

"Fair enough, Ken. Hop in and belt up!"

Oof, that sounded offensive, but I think Ken knew what I meant. There's a wry smile on his face as he secures his seatbelt.

"May I have a sweetie, John?"

Ken has noticed my packet of Werther's which I foolishly failed to stow in the glove compartment of my car.

Oof, I've just realised – Ken Worthington may now be sitting in your lap. How so? Well, before Ken arrived, I invited you into my car, didn't I? And if you accepted my invitation, presumably you chose to sit in the seat I offered, which was the front passenger seat. For all those who did that, may I offer my sincere apologies that Ken's bottom – well, his loon pants – are now touching your trousers or your skirt. You'll be fine as far as Worksop, I should think. He's not a heavy chap, after all…

Back to the Werthers. They're currently residing in the footwell of Ken's seat (formerly YOUR seat!), but, luckily, Ken – being short in the leg – hasn't trod on them yet. But I notice he's stretching his foot out as far as possible in an attempt to steer the sweetie bag with his shoe towards him, so he can, presumably – when the sweets are sufficiently close – bob down and grab them.

"Oof, Ken, careful you don't puncture the sweetie bag with your Cuban heels!"

"Don't be silly, John. There, I've got them!"

"Well done, Ken, and although I didn't answer your question, the answer is yes – please do have a sweetie."

"Thanks, John!"

"All I ask in return is that you don't crunch into it too quickly, like Mary does. Please suck the sweet for as long as possible."

"Fear ye not, John. To crunch into anything with my dentures would be perilous."

"Oof, I see."

"I shall be sucking on it for a long, long time."

"Delighted to hear that, Ken, and lovely you could join us, after all."

I've just realised that while a Werther's or travel mint will stave off boredom for a short while, if driving fatigue really takes hold I may have to pull into Doncaster North Services off the M18/M180 for a comfort break and a coffee. "In that eventuality, what type of coffee will you plump for, John?" you may ask. Well, oof, now, you've put me on the spot, dear reader. Thirty years ago, I would almost certainly have ordered an instant, preferably Mellow Birds. Twenty-five years ago it would have been a 'Campacinno', with its luxurious and frothy finish (as long as Brenda was back from her break, because back then Brenda was the only one who knew how to work the coffee machine!). But oh-ho-ho… how the world has moved on.

Now everybody has the posh coffee, especially at garages and service stations where large machines make it for you automatically. And everyone knows how to use them. But just a few years ago we were clueless. Those stirrers, for instance – they look like super-thin lolly sticks – would have left us baffled. No one would have twigged that their job was to stir the coffee – how could they with such a tiny surface area? We'd have scratched our heads for a while at those machines before giving up and sheepishly ordering an instant coffee from the Little Chef next door.

Fifteen years ago they invented the 'Late' and Mary and I switched to that one from the 'Campacinno' because it was a few pence cheaper, but reluctantly at first. Not just because it lacked the luxurious finish of the 'Campo', but because of its name – 'Late'. Our fears have proved groundless and the Late arrives just as quickly as other types of coffee. If anything, slightly quicker, because there's no frothy finish to create or chocolate dusting to apply. Oof, I miss those luxury touches, and ultimately may have to go back to the Campacinno, never mind the few extra pence.

But now, there's a new kid on the block called, erm… a flat white, I think that's right? The advantage with this type of coffee is you just say "a flat white, please" in your own natural voice (no Italian accent required). If the flat white hasn't come to your town or village yet – don't panic, it soon will. At first, it was only posh people who ordered that one, like artists with neckerchiefs and possibly a big floppy hat. But before long, ordinary members of the public (including working families) began to order it.

Joan Chitty has been known to order a flat white. The reason I know is I was with her and Mary a few months ago in our local coffee shop (the sort of place that thinks it's sophisticated but how can it be – they've still not finished plastering the walls!) and I distinctly heard Joan say to the lass serving, "A flat white and a rocky road, please, ducky." Just like that! I couldn't believe what I was hearing. It was said with such confidence it made me look at Joan in a new light (for a few minutes anyway). I'd never heard of a rocky road, let alone a flat white. I've heard of a rock cake, of course. They seemed to be everywhere when I was a kiddiewink (you could often buy one with a cup of tea at a jumble sale or garden fete), but in recent years rock cakes have inexplicably fallen out of favour, would you not agree, readers? It's true, the rocky road is the new kid on the block. Get over it – it's called progress!

"Ken? You enjoy a flat white, do you not…?"

Oof, Ken's nodded off. I wonder why? The gentle rocking motion of my Y Reg as it speeds towards the east coast would have induced slumber in Ken, but we're still parked in my drive, so there must be another reason. Maybe sucking the Werther's has exhausted Ken? Ah well… I'll not disturb him till Mary and Joan arrive, and that won't be long now as I can see them at the front door with their bags.

Hmm… I might order a flat white myself next time I'm in the arcade, although I'd be shelling out a few pence more than for the Campo (and a lot more than if I was having a Late!). Oof, and there'll be no chocolate dusting on the flat white, *and* they're served in a smaller cup, so I might not bother, actually… Mind you, *any* coffee will be very pricey in the Services, so I'll probably just have a drink from my flask – unless Ken's buying. Oof, here they come.

"Are we ready for the off now, Mary? Ken's fallen asleep waiting for you two."

"Change of plan. We're not coming to Mablethorpe, John. Doreen Melody's just invited me and Joan to a hotel near Matlock for a spa day of luxury treatments. Her daughter and her friend couldn't go, you see. Doreen's picking us up shortly in her campervan. You don't mind, do you?"

"Oh, I see. No, that's fine, Mary. I'm sure you'll have a lovely time."

"Oo, we will. Mary, are you going to have hot stone therapy or a mud experience?"

"Oo, I don't know, Joan. Ta-ta, love. You've got Ken to keep you company, I see. You'll have a great time. Come on, Joan!"

"Alright, Mary. I'm sorry I'm not going to the seaside with you, John. Bring me back a big bag of doughnuts!"

"Come on, Joan, Doreen's arriving in her campervan!"

Oof, so Mary and Joan are going to be travelling in Doreen Melody's campervan and visiting the beautiful spa town of Matlock. Suddenly Mablethorpe doesn't seem quite so alluring.

"What are you going on about, John?"

"Aha, Ken, welcome back. I hope you enjoyed your snooze?"

"I did, thank you. Are we on the A1111 yet?"

"Not quite, Ken."

Oof, you might think that Ken has used too many ones there, but he hasn't. The A1111 is indeed a road which leads to Sutton-on-Sea itself. As you'd expect, I've written a song in praise of the road, and although we're still parked up in my driveway in Sheffield, singing it may get us in the mood for the journey. Feel free to join in, readers!

The A1111

I'm on a road in Lincolnshire
That winds o'er hill and valley
Well, it would if it wasn't in Lincolnshire
Which isn't very hilly
In fact, it's flat as a pancake
But not as sweet and crispy
No time to rest, I'm on a quest
I hope my wife won't miss me

Having fun, fun, fun, fun, fun
On the A one one one one
Like the A1 but four times as good
It's the A one one one one

I'm on a road in Lincolnshire
I wouldn't take normally
But I have to get to Sutton-on-Sea
To visit a friend's beach chalet
All around me bungalows
And caravan parks entice me
I'll be sad to leave this colourful road
For the drab B1190

Having fun, fun, fun, fun, fun
On the A one one one one
Like the A1 but four times as good

It's the A one one one one

(Join in everybody, especially if you're sitting on the back seat of my Y Reg, or even on the front seat with Ken sat upon your knee!)

We're having fun, fun, fun, fun, fun
On the A one one one one
Like the A1 but four times as good
It's the A one one one one

"It's the A1111! John, that was lovely, but I feel like I've had sufficient fun for one day. May I suggest that we postpone the trip to Mablethorpe for another day? After all, you only checked my chalet last month. It's a long round trip for such an elderly vehicle. We could go next week in my Honda Civic?"

"Oof, Ken, are you suggesting my Austin Ambassador Y Reg is not up to a seaside jaunt? But you may be right. Besides, I don't know about you, but I'm getting decidedly peckish. How about lunch at the garden centre?"

"Oh yes, John, a wonderful idea! We could have soup of the day and help ourselves to a roll from the basket."

"Oof, fantastic! And after lunch, Ken, you could visit the Hansel and Gretel chalet while I sit on the garden swing and study the bronze Buddha, and even, erm… send a WhatsApp message to Mary to check if she's having a nice time at the spa. Oof, that's a sign of the times – I wouldn't have done that twenty years ago, before we were all connected on the Super Duper Highway."

"You're not wrong, John... In fact, you're right!"

"Thanks, Ken… and after the garden centre we can go for a leisurely drive around God's Own County. We can park up somewhere rural and talk to a horse in a field."

"Oo, lovely! But where's God's Own County, John? Is it far?"

"It's where we are, yer nana. South Yorkshire!"

"Oh, I see. Come on then, John, let's go!"

"Oof, Ken… exciting!"

Scenes from South Yorkshire

Follow that stream
See that chimney lean
Eat your ice cream
Where have those sandals been?
I'll go for the green
Are you watching closely, Dean?

Catch that train
Meet a soldier called Shane
Get off that train
Get back on it again
Avoid that rain
Buy some flowers for Elaine

And pubs and clubs
The bus to Crookes
And scouts and cubs
And Dobermann pups
And woodland paths
And parks and cafes
A shandy Bass in a lady's glass

Did you hear about Ryan?
It's true he was lying
Did you hear about Dale?

His computer's for sale
Did you hear about Lorna?
She's opened a sauna

And pubs and clubs
The bus to Crookes
And scouts and cubs
And Dobermann pups
And woodland paths
And parks and cafes
A shandy Bass in a lady's glass

RBM PRESENTS

'Hilarious, affectionate... gloriously banal detail'
MUZIK MAGAZINE

'A ludicrously compelling night out'
EVENING STANDARD

JOHN SHUTTLEWORTH'S BACK

'Always a delight... wrings comedy from his every grimace, shuffle or sigh'
THE GUARDIAN

www.shuttleworths.co.uk

TOUR 2020

@johnshuttlewrth

31. One Foot in the Gravy

Shame we didn't make it to Mablethorpe. Besides the funfair and doughnuts, I was hoping to find a reservoir so I could check the level. Perhaps I've never looked hard enough, but they don't seem to have many reservoirs over there on the east coast. If so, is it because they know within a few years it'll *all* be under water? Surely not, but that's what our Karen reckons – she's gone a bit environmentally self-conscious, and I reckon that's where the eating of all that pestio comes from.

But it would be a terrible shame if Karen's right and it gets flooded everywhere. For one thing, all the horses in the fields would have to learn to swim. Hang on, they *can* swim – I used to see them in Western films when I was kid, crossing a badly swollen river. John Wayne guided them over. So, panic over... Mind you, as Ken has just suggested, why don't we help save the world anyway by singing my environmental song 'One Foot in the Gravy' which – as it happens – I wrote years before climate change was invented. It's the same with mental health issues – they hadn't been thought of either – and everybody was happy, all day long!

One Foot in the Gravy

You may be blessed
With hairs upon your chest
And an ox-like constitution
But if Mother Natures's kind
Not so Father Time
He always gets his retribution

We're hurtling towards the grave
And no one's going to be saved
Folks, we've got to be brave
As we hurtle towards the grave

Famine and disease
The disappearing trees
Is it such a lovely world we're living in?
Here comes another flood
I wonder if we should
Be glad that we're not here for long, just visiting?

We're hurtling towards the grave
And no one's going to be saved
Folks, we've got to be brave
As we hurtle towards the grave

Enjoy your life
Talk kindly to your wife

Or your husband, if you happen to be a lady
Don't eat too many chips
Go on lots of day trips
Don't live with one foot in the gravy

We're hurtling towards the grave
And no one's going to be saved
Folks, we've got to be brave
As we hurtle towards the grave

(Oof, that's a bit depressing that one – apologies, readers! Let's follow that immediately with something a bit more cheerful. This next song contains some clever word play and I like to think it is the ultimate travel song!)

I Have Been to Havant

I can go to Cannock
I cannot go to Cannes

(I haven't got a passport, you see…)

I have been to Havant
For the funeral of my gran
I often walk to Walkley
For me it's not too far
But I'd be tottering to Totteridge
If I didn't take the car

I couldn't skip to Skipton
I wouldn't walk to Wick
I'd have to run to Rotherham
If my relatives were sick

(But only if they were very ill – we don't like them, as you know)

You can bring me to Bingley
You can lead me to Leeds
You can ship me to Shipley
But watch out for the weeds!

"The weeds, John?"

"On the canal, Ken. There's weeds growing that could hamper the progress of your narrow boat."

"Oh, I see!"

"Final verse, join in everybody!"

New York I have visited
Melbourne I've been near
New York in Lincolnshire
Melbourne in Derbyshire
The world is a big place
The imagination vaster
So just think of where you want to be
You'll get there faster

"I want to be on a beach in Barbados with a beautiful lady!"

"Oof, Ken… you do have some funny desires!"

"Well, where would you ideally like to be?"

"That's easy – on the sturdy chrome ladder of Doreen Melody's campervan!"

It's true, readers. And I suspect many of you were as disappointed as I not to go off with Mary and Joan in Doreen's campervan in the previous chapter. We could have parked up and had a brew, before scaling the ladder and checking the roof for 'demetrius'. (This is the word Ken always says, but I'm not sure it's right. I reckon it's 'detritirust'?) And then, erm… come down the ladder again. It would have been amazing. But guess what? We *can* do just that, and it will be a fine and fitting way to end this book. "But how can we, John?" you cry. Be patient, readers. You'll discover how very shortly...

I recently found an old audio cassette in my loft. Initially, I believed it be the greatest hits of Clodagh Rogers and was punching the air in anticipation of hearing Clodagh's finest work once again. But when I played the tape I realised I must have taped over the classy Irish chanteuse (sincere apologies, Clodagh!) with a broadcast of one of my radio shows on the snooty channel – BBC Radio 4 – back in the late nineties. The broadcast features a romantic minibreak Mary and I took in a campsite near Hope in Derbyshire – and documents the fabulous time we had. Or did we?

Judge for yourselves, because the radio show has been transcribed and typed out – not by me, I hasten to add. It's a good few years since I enjoyed access to the typewriter at the halfway house (I'd borrow it in return for me mowing their lawn, you see). Luckily, Ken Worthington knows a typist called Gillian, who he met on a coach trip to Castle Howard in 1995. Gillian works part-time as a receptionist for a skip hire company in Mexborough, and kindly agreed to type out the words of my radio show during her lunch break. "Thanks a million, Gillian!" Oof, that rhymes! I can feel a new song brewing!

Thanks for reading my book. I trust you've enjoyed it, not to mention Kevin Baldwin's brilliant and charming comic drawings? I hope also that you found the QR code hidden in one of them. Remember, the code gives you free and unfettered access to my live show in 2022. If you've not yet found it – keep looking. It's there somewhere in one of Kev's drawings, I promise!

Oof, it's like we've come full circle. "How so?" you earnestly enquire. Well, the book began with a tale all about the day I thought Ken was the devil, and the live show I just mentioned took place in a Derbyshire cavern known (rather impolitely) as the Devil's Arse. (I prefer to call it 'Satan's Bottom' and suggest you do too!)

I hope you enjoyed my crumbly selection of songs and stories, although this final one, I think you'll agree… takes the biscuit!

32.
Caravan Capers

(Birdsong. Suburban sounds.)

JOHN: Good morning! I'm standing at the rear of Doreen Melody's campervan at the foot of the sturdy chrome ladder which gives direct access to the roof. Or does it? Let's find out, shall we?

(Sound of John climbing a ladder.)

JOHN: Ah! Yes, it does! I'm on the roof! Ha! I'm not sure what to do now I'm here because... it's just a roof! Can't believe it. The ladder promised so much, didn't it? Phooh... I've been duped.

(Theme music plays.)

VOICEOVER: We present *The Shuttleworths*. Episode Four: Caravan Capers.

(Music fades out.)

JOHN: I beg your pardon. I spoke too soon! There's plenty to do up here. I can check the seal on the tinted skylight, which I have done, and it's fine; no problems there. Also, being so high up enables me to get a more accurate weather picture than I would at ground level.

And I need to know the forecast because we're going away, as you may have gathered, in this campervan, and our thanks go to Doreen for lending it us at short notice. It's a romantic weekend for two – me and Mary – to the picturesque village of Hope, Derbyshire, in celebration of our silver wedding anniversary. Two months late because there was a cock-up. You see, we were all set to go and see The Spinners at Goole Art Centre, and then at the last minute Joan Chitty approached Mary with a spare ticket to see Michael Bolton and Mary practically bit Joan's hand off. It was quite upsetting to see. And it meant I had to go and watch The Spinners alone! And I had a terrible time, 'cause I had to eat me tub on me own in the interval, which was a humiliating experience... I don't know if you've ever had to do that? I ended up facing into an alcove, pretending to read literature about forthcoming events. But that's all in the past now: it's a new day and it's a lovely day, as I can verify from my observations. So I'm going to get down the ladder now... Ooh, there's somebody at the foot of the ladder!

KEN: 'ello!

JOHN: I'll give you three guesses who it is!

KEN: Morning, John!

John climbs down the ladder.

JOHN: Right then. Eh, what you doing?

KEN: Oh, is it my turn now, John?

JOHN: No... Ken! He's trying to mount the ladder.

KEN: Hmm!

JOHN: And I won't allow it, Ken. Not dressed like that.

KEN: Why not – eh?

JOHN: Because you've got your dressing gown on and presumably there's pyjamas underneath?

KEN: Yes!

JOHN: Slippers... which are without a heel!

KEN: Mmm...?

JOHN: It's the slip-on type, favoured by ladies.

KEN: Ooh, ducky!

JOHN: I know it's only half past seven in the morning...

KEN: Mmm...?

JOHN: But I'd be a fool to let you climb that ladder, Ken...

KEN: Aw!

JOHN: ... dressed as you are.

KEN: Ooh!

JOHN: What you doing now?

(Sound of foot pump.)

JOHN: He's trying to pump the tyres up, which is what I was doing before I was distracted by the ladder.

KEN: Ooh, come on!

JOHN: He's going to have a job – it's a double-cylinder model. There'll be fierce resistance...

Ken's foot slips off the pump.

KEN: Oww!

JOHN: Oof! Sure enough, he's fallen!

KEN: Ow!

JOHN: His dressing gown's riding up... a bit ungainly for Ken.

KEN: Oof!

JOHN: Ooh, no, he's back on his feet!

KEN: Oohoo!

JOHN: A rapid recovery!

John's wife, Mary, appears.

MARY: John, have you not finished them tyres yet?

JOHN: Ooh!

MARY: Come on!

JOHN: Alright, love.

KEN: Heehee!

John takes over with the foot pump.

JOHN: (stops pumping) That'll do. See you, Ken. Oo, he's gone... I think we're ready, love!

MARY: Ooh, at last!

JOHN: Yep...

(Jaunty keyboard music starts and John starts singing. Mary joins in.)

'Caravan Capers'

JOHN: *The house plants have been watered*

We've cancelled the milk and papers!

MARY: That's right

JOHN: *If anyone calls*

Say we're on our hols

Indulging in caravan capers!

MARY: We've bolted the doors and windows...

JOHN: That was my job...

Bid farewell to neighbours!

JOHN AND MARY: *It's time to take*

A well earned break

And embark on caravan capers!

JOHN: *Oh, how long will it take us?*

MARY: *What rural thrills await us?*

JOHN: *I long to be at the water tap enjoying banter...*

With a fellow camper...

MARY: *Caravan capers...*

Well, slow down, love. There's no rush.

JOHN: Yep, pass me a mint, please, love...

MARY: Mmm, alright.

JOHN: Thank you!

(Music ends.)

Sometime later. They're still driving.

MARY: (relaxed) Mmm...

JOHN: (also relaxed) Ah! Ooh, haha!

MARY: What's the matter?

JOHN: I've not seen that before – have you, love?

MARY: What?

JOHN: Doreen's got a gonk in her back window!

Mary gasps.

JOHN: It's quite lifelike!

MARY: John!

JOHN: Bouncing about...

MARY: IT'S KEN!

JOHN: Ken!

The campervan stops abruptly. John and Mary get out and rush to the ladder at the back.

MARY: Ken?

JOHN: You alright?

KEN: (feebly) Hello, John. Mary.

MARY: Pwoah...

JOHN: Help me down with him, love.

MARY: Yep.

KEN: Oww!

JOHN: That's it, Ken. Just lie there.

MARY: Yeah.

JOHN: 'Til we get you to the hospital.

MARY: You alright, Ken?

KEN: Yes...

JOHN: (to audience) What an idiot Ken Worthington was.

Instead of viewing our departure from the comfort of his lounge, curiosity got the better of Ken and surreptitiously he'd scaled the forbidden ladder; hoping, no doubt, to alight before we'd driven off. But Ken's unsuitable footwear had hampered his attempts to disembark, and he'd had to endure a ten-mile drive over, at times, difficult terrain. In his pyjamas! But Ken's plight seemed to have cheered Mary up. She kept passing him drinks of tea from our flask!

MARY: There you go, Ken.

KEN: Thanks, Mary!

JOHN: I, too, was enjoying transporting an invalid. 'Cause I've always dreamed of being a paramedic. Don't know if you knew that... and I was a teeny bit disappointed when he suddenly said he felt better and began browsing through our campsite brochure.

(The music for 'Caravan Capers' resumes.)

KEN: Mmm!

(Ken chuckles.)

JOHN: What?

(Ken sings.)

KEN: *The campsite sounds amazing...*

JOHN: Yes... (sings) *the facilities are wide-ranging!*

MARY: Mmm, yeah.

JOHN: *Although we may, throughout our stay*
Be surrounded by animals grazing!

MARY: Oof!

KEN: Ooh!

MARY: You didn't tell me that, John.

KEN: Oohoo!

JOHN: Did I not, love?

MARY: No.

JOHN: Ooh...

KEN: *With baa-ing lambs to wake us...*
How happy our stay will make us!

JOHN: *A leisurely groom in the gents' washroom...*

KEN: *And then a hearty...*

JOHN AND MARY: *Caravan capers...*

KEN: *Full English breakfast...*

JOHN AND MARY: *Caravan capers...*

KEN: Oh! Wonderful!

JOHN AND MARY: *Caravan capers...*

KEN: Hmm-hmm! *Caravan capers!*

JOHN: Eh, Ken, don't get too excited.

KEN: Why not?

JOHN: Well, you're not coming. This break's for me and Mary!

KEN: Let me come, John!

JOHN: No way, Ken.

KEN: I'll sleep on the roof!

JOHN: You will not, Ken.

KEN: Underneath then!

JOHN: No! It's illegal.

John grabs Ken's wrist firmly.

KEN: Ow!

JOHN: Now, we've enjoyed your company, Ken, but it's time for you to go home now...

KEN: Oww...

JOHN: ... and get washed and dressed and ready for the day.

MARY: That's right.

JOHN: There's a bus stop here and here's your bus fare.

KEN: Alright...

JOHN: Alright?

KEN: Thank you...

JOHN: Good luck to you, Ken.

MARY: Bye, Ken!

KEN: Oof... ahh!

MARY: Ooh dear.

JOHN: What's the matter, Ken?

KEN: Oh... oh... I feel dizzy, John.

JOHN: (to audience) Ken's feeble attempt to open the sliding door had left him exhausted and within seconds he was in a deep slumber, from which we couldn't wake him. We had no option but to take him with us to the caravan site, though I wasn't happy about that. Well, would you be? You know, when you're having a romantic break with your wife, you don't want your neighbour tagging along. Luckily, Ken befriended a little lad from the next caravan and began playing frisbee with him, which allowed Mary to have a lie down whilst I ventured to the water tap.

(Sound of water running.)

JOHN: Where is everybody? I want to exchange banter with somebody, but everybody seems to be in their caravans watching telly! Which is fair enough, I suppose, when you're on holiday. But I brought me map with me, so I can explain to someone how I got here. Just something I like to do.

KEN: Oo!

JOHN: Oops! Ken's frisbee's just hit one of the static caravans...

KEN: That was your fault, Gavin!

JOHN: And the lady's coming out! Oohoo, Ken's for it now!

KEN: Joyce!

JOYCE: Hello, Ken.

KEN: Hello!

JOHN: It *is* Joyce! The lady who did Ken's garden a few weeks ago. That's right: he said she lived in Hope...

KEN: (in the background) I forgot you lived here, love...

JOHN: Likes gardening but doesn't have a garden! Got a little fence though. I've written a song about her, which I could play you. I'll just sit on the stile...

(Music begins.)

JOHN: 'Cause I've got me keyboard with me, in case I get inspired.

(John sings, 'She Lives In Hope'.)

She lives in Hope
Though she used to live in Barnsley,
She took bereavement calmly
And decided to relocate
She lives in Hope

And she's very keen on gardening,

She doesn't have a garden

Though she does have a garden gate!

She lives all alone

In the shadow of the peak

And when she finds herself on Lose Hill,

She only need turn to Win Hill

To recover from defeat

She lives in Hope

Though she's nothing to live in Hope for

But she knows she's got to cope, or

Join her husband, Pete

She lives in Hope...

(Music ends.)

Later that evening. John and Mary are playing cards.

JOHN: Ah, there! I've trumped you, love.

MARY: Ooh, yep.

JOHN: Yep.

Mary sighs.

JOHN: It's the evening now... just had a lovely meal.

MARY: Mmm!

JOHN: With a bottle of wine...

MARY: Yep.

JOHN: There's a little bit left actually...

MARY: Ooh!

JOHN: Which we can take home with us.

MARY: Toof... Come on, it's your go.

John puts a card down and waits for Mary.

JOHN: Some people would maintain that Knock-Out Whist is better with three players...

MARY: Mmm...

JOHN: But they're misguided, in my opinion, because with two you don't get knocked out very easily, 'cause you get a Dog's Life and then a Cat's Life. You've got a Dog's Life, haven't you, Mary?

MARY: Mmm...

JOHN: Yeah.

MARY: Yep!

JOHN: Oh, we've had a fantastic day. Really have. Went for a little stroll around the perimeter of the caravan site, didn't we, love?

MARY: Mmm!

JOHN: Spending quality time with each other...

MARY: Mmm...

JOHN: ...which is the purpose of this weekend, and it's a lovely irony that a few yards away in another caravan, Ken and Joyce are doing exactly the same thing. Enjoying a candlelit supper for two.

(Mary sighs.)

JOHN: We wish them well in their relationship. Certainly all the initial signs point to...

MARY: Oh, can you shut up, John, please. I'm trying to concentrate!

JOHN: Well, can you hurry up, please, love? You've only got two cards to choose from. It's hardly the decision of a lifetime, is it?

MARY: (pointedly) No, I took that one 25 years ago!

JOHN: (distracted) Hey... listen!

MARY: Ooh!

JOHN: Did you hear that, love?

MARY: I did, yes!

JOHN: Someone on the roof!

MARY: There is! Go on.

JOHN: Right... pass us that bottle, love. I might need to defend myself.

MARY: Mmm! Be careful, love.

John climbs campervan ladder as sinister music plays.

(Sound of an owl screeching.)

JOHN: Who's there?

(Music changes tone.)

JOHN: Oh, Ken! What you doing on me roof?

KEN: Keep your voice down, John!

JOHN: Why?!

KEN: I'm hiding from Joyce!

JOHN: What for?

KEN: Well...

JOHN: Eh?

KEN: I criticised the pudding, and I asked her to pin back the tassles...

JOHN: Eh?

KEN: You know, that hang in the door...

JOHN: Mmm...

KEN: 'Cause they were getting in me face and hair...

JOHN: Oo!

KEN: And, um...

JOHN: Ken...

KEN: She just came at me with the bottle opener...

JOHN: Ooh...

KEN: But I'm frightened, John. Genuinely.

JOHN: Yeah...

KEN: You know.

JOHN: Well, I can see that, Ken.

KEN: Mmm!

JOHN: And I'd like to say that you're safe now...

KEN: Mmm...

JOHN: But you're not.

KEN: No!

JOHN: 'Cause being so high up, you're exposed. We need to find a sheltered position for you, Ken.

KEN: Well, hurry! She's by the shower block!

JOHN: Ooh... ah! Of course!

KEN: What?

JOHN: The skylight!

KEN: Oho!

JOHN: It's already partially open...

KEN: Yes!

JOHN: Help me, Ken.

(Sound of John and Ken struggling.)

JOHN: Oh! That's it – in you go!

KEN: (slipping down) Ooh!

MARY: Ooh...

JOHN: Blimey, he's landed straight in me seat!

KEN: (happily) Hello, Mary.

MARY: Hello, Ken.

JOHN: He's even picked up the cards...

MARY: You alright?

JOHN: ... that I had. He's carrying on the game for me...

KEN: What's trumps?

JOHN: ... which is very generous of him.

MARY: Hearts.

JOHN: I've no doubt I'll be joining them in a minute, 'cause despite what I said, Knock-Out Whist is probably better with three.

MARY: You can have a drink if you want, Ken?

JOHN: But first I must find out the weather forecast, because tomorrow we're going to the Heights of Abraham!

KEN: John?

JOHN: What's the matter, Ken?

KEN: Er, can you pass the wine, please?

JOHN: (not pleased) Yes!

John passes the bottle through the skylight.

KEN: Thank you!

JOHN: Oof...

(Theme music begins.)

KEN: There you go, Mary. Cheers!

MARY: Yep. Cheers, Ken... thank you!

KEN: Mmmhmm!

JOHN: Ooh...

KEN: Here's to a lovely holiday!

JOHN: Oof!!

(Theme music plays.)

VOICEOVER: *The Shuttleworths* was written and performed by Graham Fellows and produced by Paul Schlesinger.

Whilst it's very flattering to be canonised by this church near Bolton, they should really have waited until I'd been dead for five years (the rule for new saints, apparently). And have I really achieved enough to become an actual saint? Mother Theresa's been waiting many years, so it just doesn't seem fair. I'm humbled by what's happened though, readers, and am truly grateful to everyone who was in on the decision!

Cheerio!

St. John Shuttleworth